Mindfulness Workbook

Simple Mindful Habits for More Positivity, More Balance and More Focus

(A Beginner's Guide to Finding Peace in a Stressful World)

Steve Madera

Published by Rob Miles

© **Steve Madera**

All Rights Reserved

Mindfulness Workbook: Simple Mindful Habits for More Positivity, More Balance and More Focus (A Beginner's Guide to Finding Peace in a Stressful World)

ISBN 978-1-990084-02-7

All rights reserved. No part of this guide may be reproduced in any form without permission in writing from the publisher except in the case of brief quotations embodied in critical articles or reviews.

LEGAL & DISCLAIMER

The information contained in this book is not designed to replace or take the place of any form of medicine or professional medical advice. The information in this book has been provided for educational and entertainment purposes only.

The information contained in this book has been compiled from sources deemed reliable, and it is accurate to the best of the Author's knowledge; however, the Author cannot guarantee its accuracy and validity and cannot be held liable for any errors or omissions. Changes are periodically made to this book. You must consult your doctor or get professional medical advice before using any of the suggested remedies, techniques, or information in this book.

Upon using the information contained in this book, you agree to hold harmless the Author from and against any damages, costs, and expenses, including any legal fees potentially resulting from the application of any of the information provided by this guide. This disclaimer applies to any damages or injury caused by the use and application, whether directly or indirectly, of any advice or information presented, whether for breach of contract, tort, negligence, personal injury, criminal intent, or under any other cause of action.

You agree to accept all risks of using the information presented inside this book. You need to consult a professional medical practitioner in order to ensure you are both able and healthy enough to participate in this program.

Table of Contents

INTRODUCTION 1

CHAPTER 1 MINDFULNESS FOR BEGINNERS 2

CHAPTER 2: RIGHT MINDFULNESS 6

CHAPTER 3: ANNIHILATE ANXIETY 17

CHAPTER 4: DEMYSTIFY MINDFULNESS 21

CHAPTER 5: HOW MINDFULNESS CHANGED MY LIFE 32

CHAPTER 6: BOARDING THE MINDFULNESS TRAIN 46

CHAPTER 7: WHERE TO BEGIN WITH MINDFULNESS 53

CHAPTER 8: THE AIR YOU BREATH 59

CHAPTER 9: PREPARATION TO MEDITATION: CULTIVATING ATTITUDES FOR MINDFULNESS 64

CHAPTER 10: MASTERING YOUR THOUGHTS 68

CHAPTER 11: FORMAL MINDFULNESS MEDITATION 77

CHAPTER 12: START WITH RELAXATION AND BREATHING 90

CHAPTER 13: ANXIETY 96

CHAPTER 14: SIMPLE FORMS OF MEDITATION 101

CHAPTER 15: MINDFULNESS MEDITATION 109

CHAPTER 16: FINDING MINDFULNESS AT WORK 116

CHAPTER 17: SPIRITUALITY 132

- CHAPTER 18: THE POWER OF GRATITUD 138
- CHAPTER 19: MINDFUL LIVING 143
- CHAPTER 20: BREAKING FREE FROM YOUR PAST 148
- CHAPTER 21: HOW MINDFULNESS HELPS WITH EVERYDAY PROBLEMS 155
- CHAPTER 22: PRACTISING BODY SCAN 164
- CHAPTER 23: MINDFULNESS FOR STRESS 172
- CHAPTER 24: BENEFITS OF NEUROPLASTICITY AND POSITIVE THINKING 178
- CHAPTER 25: WHEN TO PRACTICE MINDFULNESS? 187
- CONCLUSION 191

Introduction

Oftentimes, we wonder how mind-body practices like meditation and yoga can change the mood of an individual, how regular physical exercises helps man to improve his memory, why damage to the brain can reflect in the transformation of human personality or how lowliness is capable of increasing the risk of heart disease in a human person. How does this work? Are these teachings truly practicable? If they are, do they really possess such significance that has been attributed to them? These are some of the questions that readily come to mind when faced with teachings of Mindfulness. To attend to these questions, let's take a study into these beliefs.

To better appreciate the topic of this paper, it is pertinent to extensively discuss the key terms found in the topic as they relate to the center message and subject matter of the paper.

Chapter 1 Mindfulness For Beginners

What is Mindfulness?

Mindfulness is simply paying attention to the present moment. It is being aware of the now, by using techniques like yoga, breathing, and meditation. Mindfulness allows you to become more aware of your thoughts and feelings so you can better manage them, instead of them overwhelming you.

Thoughts and feelings, not just the negatives but also the positives, can overwhelm you if you don't know how to handle them. Mindfulness can give you the non-judgmental awareness of your feelings, thoughts, and even your sensations. It is allows you to directly know what is going on inside you, as well as outside, in every moment.

Western medicine just caught the principles in the late 1970's, but Buddhist monks have been practicing the principles of mindfulness for over 2,000 years.

Why You Should Practice Mindfulness

In a nutshell, mindfulness helps improve both your physical and mental health and it helps you to deliberately pay attention to your feelings, thoughts, and sensations without judgment.

You live in a busy world, a world where you need to care for the kids, the house, and maintain a career, a world where you are expected to provide for your family, or a world where you need to study hard, get a job, and help improve the lives of your family. In this day and age, you cannot be caught doing nothing or the world will swallow you whole.

Are you one of those who live in the fast lane? Are you one of those whose relaxation has been relegated to last priority because you have a lot to take care of? The practice of mindfulness would help you get back to the basics without compromising the things that you need to do on a daily basis.

Mindfulness and Your Physical Health

Mindfulness can do all these for your physical health:

Relaxation

Relieves stress

Lowers high blood pressure

Improves sleep

Improves blood circulation

Reduces chronic pain

Helps prevent and treat heart disease

Helps ease alleviate gastrointestinal difficulties

Mindfulness and Your Mental Health

Expert psychotherapists have been using mindfulness over the years to help in the treatment of some of the most common mental problems, such as:

Anxiety disorder

Depression

Drug and alcohol abuse

Obsessive Compulsive Disorder

Marital/relationship conflicts

Experts believe that mindfulness also helps people to accept different life experiences, especially when they are subjected to tragic situations and/or painful events, rather than "running away" from them or being wary in dealing with them.

Chapter 2: Right Mindfulness

The Dhamma, according to the Buddha, is the ultimate truth of things and is directly timeless, visible, and calling out to be seen and acted upon. The Buddha claims that the Dhamma is always available to every person; thus, it is realizable within oneself.

Sati, which is translated as "mindfulness" is a mental faculty, which brings the experience field into focus and makes it available to insight. As mentioned in the previous sections, mindfulness refers to awareness, attentiveness, or presence of mind. However, awareness involved in mindfulness is extremely different from the awareness that an individual displays during the usual mode of consciousness. While all consciousness requires awareness in terms of experiencing or knowing an object, the kind of awareness applied in the practice of mindfulness is at a special level. This level is referred to as the bare attention, which is a detached observation of what transpires within an individual and around him in the present moment.

During the practice of right mindfulness, one's mind is trained to stay in the present moment, being quiet, open, and alert while reflecting what is currently happening. This means that all interpretations as well as judgments should be suspended. Should interpretations and judgments come up during the practice of right mindfulness, they should be simply registered, then dropped.

The practice of right mindfulness is to take note of everything as it occurs. This is comparable to a surfer riding the waves on the sea. Right mindfulness is simply riding the changes in the events transpiring in the present moment. The entire practice is a process of coming back into the present moment without being distracted with thoughts and without slipping away.

Mindfulness employs a persuasive grounding function. It secures one's mind in the present in order to avoid slipping away into the past or the future with his regrets, hopes, fears, and memories. Without mindfulness, the mind would be similar to a pumpkin when placed on a pond's surface. It floats away and would only remain on the surface of the water. However, the mind founded in mindfulness is similar to a stone, which stays where it is and sinks into the water, reaching the bottom of the pond. Strong mindfulness allows the mind to stay focused on its object and goes into its characteristics profoundly.

Four Foundations of Mindfulness (Cattaro Satipatthana)

Right mindfulness is developed or cultivated through the four foundations of mindfulness or cattaro satipatthana, which is a practice involving the mindful contemplation of four objective spheres, including the body, states of mind, feelings, and phenomena.

According to the Buddha, the four foundations of mindfulness lead the only way to attaining purity, ending grief and pain, overcoming lamentation and sorrow, realizing of Nibbana (Nirvana), and entering the right path. These foundations are referred to as "the only way" or ekayano maggo, which entails that the attainment of freedom can only happen through penetrating the field of experience through the practice of the right mindfulness.

The contemplation of the body is one of the four objective spheres and applications of mindfulness. It is focused with the existence's material side. The other objective spheres are concerned with the existence's mental side. All four contemplations are required to complete the practice of right mindfulness.

In general, the body is the first contemplation sphere to be taken up although there is no fixed order as to what sphere comes first. The other three spheres may be taken up later when mindfulness is strong and clear enough.

Mindfulness Meditation in the Buddhist Context

Mindfulness meditation, based on Buddhism, has three central purposes. These include knowing the mind, training the mind, and freeing the mind.

Knowing the Mind

Most people spend their hours, days, or even their whole lives caught up with concerns, activities, and thoughts just because it is easy to do so. Indeed, a great number of people dwell in their thoughts and actions, mostly negative, instead of understanding why they operate the way they do. Most people are clueless with regard to their motivation, thoughts, and the nature of their feelings and reactions. In mindfulness practice, the first step is to discern oneself in terms of what goes on in the mind, body, and emotions as well as the underlying tendencies that operate within.

Knowing the mind is a part of mindfulness practice, which is a simple discovery process. It does not involve judgments, but a meditative discovery that calls for stillness. An individual's level of stillness serves as a backdrop, which highlights what is transpiring. An agitated mind is easy to notice and does not call for too much stillness. Thus, discovery entails familiarity. For instance, being familiar with what an agitated mind is, translates discovery. It is knowing what the mind is and its effect on one's body. Discovery is becoming familiar with the emotions, belief, and thoughts are present.

The aspect of knowing in mindfulness is conscious and deliberate. A presence of mind develops when you know how something works. It is clearly knowing that you know. For instance, you and a friend are a part of an unruly crowd. Both of you are not caught up in the agitation of the crowd. If you have the knowing aspect of mindfulness, there will be a hint of recognition, say, a smile passing between you and your friend as you know that you are not caught up in the agitation.

When it comes to knowing the mind, you only focus on knowing instead of attempting to change what is happening.

Observing the mind results in a relief and a radical change, especially for those who are inclined to always make something happen.

Training the Mind

The mind is a process. It involves a series of processes that interact with each other. Therefore, it is not static, but pliable and easily influenced. However, you can train and shape the mind. One significant part of the Buddhist's practice of mindfulness meditation involves taking responsibility for the activities and tendencies of the mind so it can work in beneficial ways. If you fail to take responsibility of your own mind, external forces will train and shape it. These forces include companions, advertisements, media, and other components of the society.

The best way to start training the mind is in compassion and kindness. When you start to explore how to be kinder, more compassionate, and more forgiving, you can avoid mental conflict with yourself, others, or the changes in your life. During the practice of mindfulness, mental conflict may be revealed, which can take the form of confusion, despair, discouragement, aversion, anger, or ambition. When you address conflict with another conflict, it will only add up to your suffering. As such, it is best to start training your mind in compassion and kindness towards yourself, others, and the changes in life.

In some cases, making too much effort during mindfulness meditation can result in a negative way. When there is too much effort, it is like escaping something, making meditation as an obligation or a penance. It also tends to measure every progress, which interferes with the true purpose of meditation. A remedy to this is to train the mind to become more at ease with the way things are. You can develop an ability to be comfortable or decompressed with what is transpiring instead of organizing the conditions of the situation.

When your mind is relaxed and experiences rest during meditation, it would be much easier to train it. You also develop mental stability or concentration.

By training the mind, you can promote the growth of ethical virtue, discernment, generosity, the capacity to avoid clinging, and courage. Buddhists usually choose a specific quality to nurture one step at a time.

Freeing the Mind

In the Buddhist practice of mindfulness meditation, it is important to train the mind to let go of clinging. Once you are done with the first aspect of Buddhist mindfulness meditation, which is knowing the mind, it will reveal where and how clinging is present. There are some painful forms of clinging, including holding on to desire, pleasure, ideals, possessions, people, judgments, and self-image. All these limit the peace and freedom of the mind.

According to the teachings of Buddhism, people can let go of clinging, and consequently, free the mind as well as the heart. In the Buddhist mindfulness meditation, the ultimate goal is to free the heart from shackles, constrictions, or barriers. This starts by taking small steps that result in a corresponding peace. The heart will be completely at peace when it is completely free. On the other hand, attaining complete freedom is not easy to attain. It calls for training and knowledge.

The three aspects of Buddhist mindfulness meditation -- knowing, training, and freeing the mind -- all develop together. Once you know yourself, it will be easy to train yourself as well as know the needs that should be let go. It will be easier to know yourself when you train your mind more. In addition, you will be able to let go of more wisdom and strength. Consequently, the more you let go, there will be lesser obstructions to understanding yourself. Ultimately, all these will make it easier to train your mind.

On the other hand, only few people care for the state of the minds as much as they care for their bodies, possessions, or clothes. Caring for one's body is an everyday task; however, few people realize that their minds also need regular care and training. In the Buddhist ways, knowing, training, and freeing the mind are ways of caring for it and at the same time having the goal of becoming free from suffering.

Chapter 3: Annihilate Anxiety

Anxiety, when reduced to the basics, is just an irrational form of fear. It is trying to tell you that something horrific **might** happen, that you **might** not be good enough, or that someone **might** be thinking poorly of you.

Anxiety stems from the evolutionary by-product of exaggerated fear. When only the strong survived, being ever-vigilant of danger was necessary to survive. It kept you on your guard. It drove you to seek shelter, food, and water.

In our world today, we don't have to worry about threats lurking around every corner. Yet, certain prehistoric parts of our brain are still prone to be afraid and anxious.

Anxiety unavoidably finds us, but rather than allowing it to develop further, we should be quick to recognize it and seek a cure.

Below are two simple mindfulness exercises for anxiety that you can easily integrate into your daily life. They don't take much time, and regular practice will make an enormous difference in your overall level of anxiety.

1). Observe a tree (5 minutes)

Choose a tree, any tree. Focus on the tree and allow your attention to be fully absorbed by it. Observe it. Notice things about its physical characteristics. For example, you could say to yourself, "I notice that this object has a broad trunk, and a fan-like leaves."

Notice textures, colors, and shapes without judging them as good or bad, pleasant or unpleasant, ugly or beautiful.

Don't assess or think about the tree. Just observe it for what it is. Do this for five minutes.

2). Observe your thoughts (15 minutes)

Find a comfortable position. You can be lying down or sitting. If you are sitting, keep you back straight. Relax your shoulders and just let them drop. Close your eyes.

Focus on your breathing. Simply be aware to how it feels like in your body as you inhale slowly and then slowly exhale. Immerse yourself completely in the experience. Spend a few minutes here. Imagine that you are "surfing the waves" of your own breath.

Next, shift your attention to your thoughts. Become alert to whatever thoughts enter your mind.

Try to view them as objects in your mind. They are just events happening inside your mind. You can imagine them as water flowing down the stream.

Notice them as they enter your consciousness, develop, and then disappear. You don't have to hold onto your thoughts, just let them occur and disappear on their own.

If at anytime you become aware that you are getting immersed in a thought, observe what took you focus away and then slowly bring your attention back to your thoughts again. Getting immersed in a thought is completely normal. Just notice it and shift your attention back to observing.

Swing your attention back to your breathing after doing a few minutes of "thought observing". Open your eyes when you are ready.

You can use your "observer mind" in any situation to slow down, step back and calm your anxiety.

Chapter 4: Demystify Mindfulness

A unique form of meditation is known as mindfulness. This simply means to bring your

attention to the present moment. Instead of thinking about the past or the future, you

bring your mind to the present moment. You don't think about what your spouse said, or

what your boss wants you to do. Instead, you focus on the task at hand. By doing this you

control your thoughts from rushing in random directions. You still have thoughts, but they are related only to the present moment.

You are allowed to think about how you feel right now, how your body feels, what each of your sense organs observes, etc. You can think about the sights, the smells, and the

sounds. You can think about whatever it is that you are doing, but you can't think about the past or the future.

This is a simple and incredibly powerful way of meditating and controlling your thoughts. It is also harder to do than it sounds. The goodness of mindfulness is the fact that you can practice it while doing anything. You can start by practicing it while taking a walk, or just

sitting quietly in a peaceful spot. Later on you can begin to stay mindful throughout the day no matter what you are doing.

It is very easy to become lost in your work when you love what you are doing. Sportsmen

and musicians talk about being in the zone, where they forget about everything else and only focus on the present moment. They'll tell you that this experience doesn't only help them perform better, but also fills them up with a kind of peace that is hard to achieve in

daily life. It is blissful and nothing short of a spiritual experience. You can practice mindfulness and have the same experience even while doing something boring or dull. You can experience it even while washing dishes if you only pay complete attention to the present moment and think of nothing else.

This type of meditation will help you release stress and become positive and happy. It

will also increase your productivity and the ability to focus and concentrate. You can try

it simultaneously as you also form a more formal meditation habit. To do this you just

have to remind yourself repeatedly through the day to pay attention to the present moment and not to think about the past or the future.

Who is it for?

We live in a world where, thanks in part to the demands of modern day life and the many

stimuli around us, our minds are never quiet. In fact, modern day life is so hectic that at

any given moment our minds are acting as never-stopping thought factories that spin

thoughts like an out-of-control carousel and, as unfortunate as it sounds, the more we try to stop these thoughts at a conscious level, the more they spin out of control.

While this is a fact of modern day life, many of us are aware that to live a good life, one

of the things we must do is attain a new level of peace and tranquility. Unfortunately,

because our hearts and minds have a tendency to concentrate on negative memories and worry about the future, instead of feeling peaceful, our regrets of the past leave us

swimming in negativity, which breeds stress, while our concerns of the future bring us anxiety. This is no way to live life.

Daily stressors are a fact we cannot escape; as such, many of us are constantly seeking effective ways to manage the stress we experience on a daily basis. If like most people,

you have done a fair bit of research on stress management strategies, you have come

across mindfulness and its potent ability to fight stress and anxiety, and wondered what it

is or how you can practice it. However, because the suggestion that you should "sit and observe your breath for 30 minutes" seems too much, until this point, you may have just toyed with the idea without giving it much thought.

Mindfulness and meditation, in general, are great for you. How many of us appreciate the

gift of the present? We all want to be successful. We all want to be happy. And this pursuit of happiness drives us to work hard and stay busy. We rush from one task to

another, struggling all the while to keep all our balls up in the air. By the time we sort out one thing, 10 new problems crop up. We lament the past, and worry about our future, and

can't stand the present. No wonder we are all so stressed out!

To relieve this stress we seek distractions. Luckily for us we live in the age of

information overload. There are distractions left, right, and center. Everyday we have to

catch up with new emails, blog feeds and news articles - a plethora of social networks fight for our attention every minute of the day. TV shows and movies help us

momentarily escape the misery of our present. Advertisements bombard us with enticing

desires, no matter where we are. Alcohol, cigarettes and drugs provide the ultimate

escape. If you can escape these addictions, you might find yourself addicted to much subtler drugs such as the sugar rush of a quick snack or the fleeting elation of buying unnecessary stuff with money you don't have.

The culture today deals with emotions and problems through distractions. This strategy

doesn't work at all and we end up with a lot of stress and disorders like depression,

attention deficit disorder, and anxiety. We've tried a lot of methods for relieving this stress.

Now a new movement is gaining momentum. It's called mindfulness and has become

very popular in corporate circles as a stress relieving technique. But mindfulness is not

just a technique to relieve the stress that emanates from a hectic lifestyle, it is an ancient

practice to live life in a way that prevents the build up of stress in the first place. The best way to combat stress is to avoid building it up to unmanageable levels.

Mindfulness can mean different things. Mindfulness meditation is a specific form of

meditation, the core of which lies in intentionally focusing one's attention in the present

moment. Mindfulness, as a practice, consists of bringing one's attention to the task at hand - no matter what task you are doing, throughout the day. As a whole, mindfulness is

a way of life. It is the philosophy that the best place to live life from is right here, right

now. In fact, most spiritual traditions talk about this very concept even though they might use different words for mindfulness such as awareness, presence, consciousness, etc.

In this book, I'll take a broader view of mindfulness that will show that it is much more than just a form of stress relief. By building the mindfulness habit, you can completely

change the way you live your life. You will receive the following benefits from

mindfulness:

- Reduced stress, anxiety and depression.

- Increased concentration and the ability to focus on the task at hand.

- Increased productivity and efficiency at work.
- More control over your life as it will become much more manageable.
- Improved mental health that can lead to improvement in physical health as well.
- The ability to enjoy every task, no matter how boring.
- A deeper understanding of your own mind and soul as you face your emotions instead of stuffing them away.

- A well-rounded personality that comes with dealing with your emotions.
- A solid character that develops when you become aware of your actions and make life decisions based on your purpose, principles and values.

Technically, mindfulness as a philosophy is just one of many 'life philosophies', but once you understand what mindfulness is all about, and you begin to practice mindfulness regularly and turn it into a habit, you'll realize that it is the only way to live. If you've ever felt overwhelmed by life, you need to try mindfulness, as it is the only solution to the enormity, complexity, and absurdity of life.

Chapter 5: How Mindfulness Changed My Life

I have been traveling the world for the last year, and I have been faced with many difficult situations. During this time, I have had the chance to let go of a lot of stress that I used to hold onto. Stress, of course, comes in many different forms, but it is ultimately our adaptability to stress that matters in the end.

My lifelong practice of yoga and meditation has helped me to live in the moment, release what has happened in the past and worry less about the future. Meditation essentially builds up our adaptability bank to stress. The more we practice, both in the present and through a daily practice, the more we can deal with stress in a calm, controlled manner.

I wasn't always practicing meditation and mindfulness as well as now. Not long ago, I had a partner that I shared my bed with, and I had to wake up early often to teach yoga or Pilates. Just the thought of waking up early was enough to give me insomnia. My struggle with sleep caused me to drink alcohol excessively and pop sleeping pills, and if I didn't have either, I would cry and pitch a fit, sometimes yelling and throwing glasses in the kitchen. I became angry that I couldn't sleep- clearly, my sympathetic nervous system was taking over and that was surely not going to help me sleep. I felt out of control.

It affected me in many ways- I was unhappy, unstable, and had gained weight. A series of events, however, lead me to travel outside of the United States for an extended period of time. My car had been totaled and I ended my last relationship and found a job in Nicaragua teaching yoga for 3 months. If I could do it you could do it too, sometimes things that people think are impossible are easier than they look.

3 months turned into 12, and now I plan my life around traveling and teaching. Yes, I still have bills to pay and I am not rich by

any means. I budget accordingly and work as I travel. I work a lot as I travel, actually. I take short-term yoga and writing freelance jobs, sometimes not sure what my next job will be, but in the meantime, I can do what I love and work on creating my own dream life.

Since I've started traveling, my sleeping habits have improved, my mood swings have decreased, my emotional instability and irritability have all but disappeared, and I lost that extra weight I had gained. Part of this I attribute to connecting back to nature- living closer to the earth. Many of the places I have lived and worked throughout the last year are in the jungle or by the beach and are not equipped with air-conditioning. The early to bed, early to rise mentality that was so difficult for me in the past is much easier when you don't live in an air-conditioned box, disconnected from the cycles of nature.

Another thing about traveling is that it forces you to be active. Often, when traveling on a budget you may not have access to a car, so walking or biking becomes a part of your daily routine. And you may even pick up some new activities or adventure sports such as surfing or hiking volcanoes. There are so many activities you can do outside, from stand up paddle boarding on a river in Costa Rica to feeding elephants in Thailand that not only challenge you but also reward you for stepping outside of your comfort zone. You may not like everything, but you may also find something you enjoy that you would have never known otherwise.

For example, I never thought I would surf. It was not my intention when I went to Nicaragua. But when I arrived, I was only teaching a few yoga classes per day and had a lot of free time. I didn't have a gym to go to or dance practice in the afternoon, and I certainly didn't want to be spending all my free time in front of my laptop or watching Netflix like I did back home. So I took up a friend's offer to teach me how to surf- and the rest is history.

I don't claim to be any good- I do it purely for enjoyment, which is actually outside my normal character. Before, if I weren't good at something right away, I would give it up. But surfing is different. And I've now surfed in 4 different countries in the past year.

And then there's hiking. I have always loved hiking but have never considered myself a hardcore hiker and have never done an overnight backpack trip. However, also in Nicaragua, I decided it would be a good idea to hike Volcán Maderas, on Ometepe Island. It is one of the hardest things I have ever done in my life. It took me nearly 10 hours.

The hike up was not as bad as the way down. Many say going downhill is easier, however, I found the opposite to be true. I had plenty of energy on the way up- but the way down was treacherous. It started to get dark on the way down, and I had to watch every step on muddy rocks to make sure I didn't fall or twist my ankle. My entire body was hurting and I was crying by the end. My fight or flight response took over and I wasn't sure I was going to make it. Luckily with the help of my guide, I did eventually make it and collapsed at the nearby farm afterward. I'm glad I did it, but I certainly tested my physical limits.

That is probably the last time I remember truly having an emotional breakdown, which had been all too common in my life before. Previously, I would be set off by the littlest things with my partner or about work, or I would feel depressed about never having enough money. But living this transient nomadic life has taught that I am always right where I am supposed to be and I have everything I need at the moment.

And if I don't have my needs covered- if I am concerned about money, food, or shelter- I can get creative to solve my problems. I've used couchsurfing to save money on hotel rooms, I've started working online to generate money when I decided to backpack through Peru on a budget, and I've learned to buy my food at local markets for so cheap I could eat lunch for a week for $5 in some places.

I've done things I never thought I would do. I renewed my passport overseas. I voted abroad. I've taught yoga in places people dream of, including my own dream locations.

I have also been traveling by myself this entire time. I have made tons of friends along the way, but most of all, my relationship with myself has deepened. I have a newfound confidence and have learned to truly love myself and accept wherever I am in the moment- whether it's eating dinner by myself or going on random adventures to waterfalls with new friends. After all is said and done, I have felt my life as a healing journey. Many of us feel broken throughout our lives and for one reason or another, that we are not good enough for …. XYZ, fill in the blank with career, relationship, etc. The truth is we must want to change ourselves from the inside out. We must know that it is a process and a transformation. Ultimately, it never ends!

Life's greatest challenges can also be your greatest rewards. If it weren't for that awful situation I was in a year ago, I would have never had the courage to step outside my comfort zone and begin teaching yoga internationally and writing full time. And I've taught in 4 countries now, in 1 year alone! I feel better and more energetic than ever and you can too with the practice of mindfulness, meditation, and a good dose of travel. While releasing expectations of the future and judgment of myself through mindfulness, I have been able to energetically shift my thinking to truly believe in all that I am capable of doing.

The biggest shift came after sitting in an ayahuasca ceremony with a shaman deep in the Amazon jungles of Peru. I showed up at my shaman's house alone, scared and exhausted from detoxing off of caffeine. There were fears in the back of my mind about what I was about to get myself into- and alone at that as a single white blonde woman at a jungle hut, about to take psychedelic drugs with strangers.

I took some deep breaths and remained calm and trusted that I was exactly where I was supposed to be. The journey to their center was not easy from their humble home, either. It took us 9 hours- a moto taxi, a shuttle van, 3 boats, and a short hike. We went down a tributary of the Amazon River that had dried up, so we had to keep downsizing boats. With little food in my system and only my 2nd day without coffee in over 10 years, I felt pretty horrible but somehow kept going.

The ayahuasca experience for me was like a deep meditation. I walked out of it with a deep passion and fervor for life that I have never experienced before. Being happy and healthy are two of the most important things I have gained from not only this experience, but also through traveling, healing myself, and pursuing what I love to do full time.

Sometimes traveling can be a shock to the system- in more ways than one. The food is different, the people are different- you are forced to be careful with what you eat, how you respond, even how you dress. Things we take for granted in our lives back home suddenly take on more meaning when we see them scarcely in other settings.

The night I arrived in Nicaragua I got food poisoning. It had been a long day of travel and stress right from the start. A mistake had been in my flight booking and when I got to the airport, I found out my flight had been made for the wrong day- a month later! How no one caught this, I don't know!

I was able to get on the next flight, thankfully, but it set my mind whirling. I was so nervous when I got to Nicaragua because of all the fear so many people had set in my mind about going there. When my driver unfortunately was nowhere to be found upon my arrival and I found a piece of equipment I had brought with me broken in the baggage claim area, I paid extra for a taxi with the female interpreter from the airport to come with me.

Needless to say, that first day was certainly stressful, and it didn't help that that night I ended up having to sleep in a un-air conditioned 12 person dorm, running to the shared bathroom all night long. My fears, as well as others, proved to be unfounded. Of course, I was always careful at night, but the things that annoyed me the most in Nicaragua were the men always yelling, "Taxi, chica?!" as I would walk by or the frequent whistles I would get walking down the street in Granada. They were always harmless.

In the end what I have found is that our perceptions of other people are often much more harmful than the people and places themselves. We build up these tough exterior bubbles and project a lot of our fear on other people. However, through this experience of cultural immersion, I have learned to soften my hard shell and let fear fall to the wayside.

There's no way you can travel long-term if you're afraid all the time. If you constantly think your tuk-tuk driver in Asia is going to kidnap you every time you go somewhere, you will constantly be unhappy. Letting go of your fears and worries through traveling experiences will help you come into a place of pure presence, a sort of emptiness that feels like anything is possible. Learning to let go and live in the moment is how you find peace and happiness. Stress blocks you from getting there.

Stress: A Silent Killer

Stress is an epidemic in Western society. Known as one of the deadliest silent killers, stress that is accumulated over time can wreak havoc on the body and mind. Constant pressure to excel and be successful in all areas of life is very real in America. From school, to work, to relationships and other extracurricular activities, the fact is, taking on too much leaves very little left over for our own self in the end.

The highest causes of stress include fears and worries about money, the economy, and work. Younger generations are more concerned about school and college debt while older generations are stressed about their retirement. On top of that, it seems that pretty much everyone is stressed out by the current state of global politics and the uncertain economic future of the world. Current polls show that 57% of Americans are chronically stressed out. That number is actually probably much higher!

Everyone knows that the news really never has much of anything positive to say. Regular media highlights crime, war, and deaths which can cause stress and for people to feel unsafe. This concern for safety adds heightened worry. While it is good to be informed about certain situations, it is actually documented that crime has been decreasing in America. The problem is, the perception of it has not, so many people today fear for their safety much more than they used to, which adds unnecessary stress.

The truth is our internal stresses do not always reflect our external world. Our minds are playing tricks on us! This ultimately prevents us from living up to our true potential. Clearly, money issues have a lot to do with stress and happiness levels. Studies have shown that homes with incomes less than $50,000 per year report higher stress levels than those who have higher incomes. But everyone seems to know someone who makes tons of money and is still stressed out. From feeling like you'll never have enough, paying off credit cards or school loans, raising kids and more, the feelings surrounding money can often turn any mood sour. While we can't make money grow on trees, we can, however, control how we feel about the situation and make small changes to improve the situation. This is where mindfulness comes in.

Chapter 6: Boarding The Mindfulness Train

Being Mindful Means Being Aware

In today's fast paced world, we sometimes forget to look before we cross roads, what happens then? We abuse others, maybe get into fights, and then curse the entire day for being such a lousy mistake. If you take a walk in the park, do you see things that you might have missed otherwise? Maybe a beautiful butterfly, maybe wet, green grass? Maybe that ripe fruit hanging for its life? If you practice mindfulness, you will be conscious of your experiences. You won't miss a thing and you'll learn to be grateful every day.

Being Mindful Means Being Attentive

If you see some people walking down the street, you'll notice humongous earphones blocking their hearing. They're so busy listening to whatever, that they can no longer hear their own heartbeats. They don't know the rhythm of their own breath. Moreover, they can't hear other people unless they're tapped on the shoulder! It's true.

Recently, while I was on the train, I met this young woman who was heading where I was heading. As soon as journey began, out came these big earphones, and from the earphones, I could hear loud music. When we reached our destination, she was unaware and wasn't paying attention; I had to nudge her so she could get to her destination. Although she was aware of the music that was playing, although she was fully attentive on the lyrics, if that awareness and attentiveness was directed to a better cause, it would bring about amazing results.

Being Mindful Means Being Able To Remember To Be Mindful

This header might have confused you, I know, but let me explain. Let's use an example of something that many men will experience: becoming a father. A good friend of mine recently became a father and it took a long while for him to adjust to his new life. He had two options when he was battling the unwanted stress that was brought on by thinking too much about things he couldn't change. His first option was to keep thinking about the future and whether he was going to be a good father or remind himself about the fact that he couldn't change the future and that he should just forget about it and enjoy today. It's much too easy to forget about being mindful, so you need to have the ability to keep reminding yourself about being aware and paying attention. But it's not easy! Sometimes, no matter how much you remind yourself about being mindful, you still fall between the gaps.

The stress keeps coming at you, the tensions keep rising. But all you have to do then is virtually lock your brain, clean the clutter, and bring your attention to your own breathing. Pay attention to your breath, the warmth, the rhythm, and the frequency and you'll see how effectively this calms you down. I recently found a quote which beautifully simplifies mindfulness, "Mindfulness is simply being aware of what is happening right now without wishing it were different; enjoying the pleasant without holding on when it changes (which it will); being with the unpleasant without fearing it will always be this way (which it won't)." – James Baraz

Respond To Your Experience, Don't React To Them

By achieving mindfulness, you will also learn how to respond to your experiences instead of reacting to them. My friend, who probably already knows he's being quoted here, will hate me for this, but for the sake of argument, let's look at his example again! You probably remember what happened to him, and I even told you he had two choices to make, but now let's take an example of him remembering that experience.

One day he stopped by with his now three year old daughter, and from out of nowhere, he remembered how he reacted the time his daughter was born. When he was talking to me about his experience, I saw how angered he was with the way he behaved. He 'reacted' to his experience with anger in the form of words and actions, when he should have 'responded' to his experience. If you react, you have no choice but to deal with that fear or anger for the rest of your life, but if you choose to respond, that fear gets archived and you prepare yourself better for similar future events, i.e. you get a choice!

It's like a glass half full/half empty situation – if you think it's half full, you're happy it's still half full, but if it's half empty, you're feeling sorry that half's gone! Apart from reacting or responding to experiences there's another thing you need to keep in mind – the ability to not pass judgment. As humans, we always have the temptation to pass judgments, whether it's on an experience or a person. We have our own likes and dislikes; we know how to judge experiences as 'good' ones or 'bad' ones.

When you ask a person what they fear, they'll have a long list of fears, but when you ask them what makes them happy, the list is somewhat shorter. There are two reasons for that: one, they don't pay enough attention to the good list or, two, they pay too much attention to the bad list. You can also achieve mindfulness if you let go of your judgments and focus on what's in front of you, whether good or bad. You should be able to see things as they are without filtering them with your personal thoughts based on your past experiences.

For example, my friend did have a 'bad' experience, but for almost all humans on earth, the birth of a child is a good experience, but suppose he has another child, if he connects that experience to his second newborn, he'd be repeating the same mistake.

Mindfulness will teach you how to open your heart to everyone and everything. This, in today's world, is a quality that many miss. If you're open-hearted, you're no longer cruel, you're no longer jealous, you're not cold or unfriendly. People who surround you will say, he/she is the most kind, most compassionate, warm, and friendly person I've ever met! Isn't this what makes a good human? If you convince yourself that you're not good at something, you will not try it, but if you accept it open-heartedly, you will not fail. Being mindful has lots of benefits, apart from forgiving friends (!) and new experiences; it's all about enjoying your life today so you don't miss out on anything you normally would ignore.

Chapter 7: Where To Begin With Mindfulness

When you are getting acquainted with being more mindful in life, you should start simple and work your way up. When you start with easier things, it is a lot more likely that you will stick to this path instead of abandoning it out of frustration. To feel more self-sufficient and motivated in this area, you must realize that mindfulness is a muscle you have to build. Beginning with paying attention and being mindful of very simple things is best.

What Exactly is Mindfulness?

Mindfulness can be seen as paradoxical because it is both as simple as can be and very difficult to achieve. An example of this would be something simple, like looking at your palm. Pay attention to the colors and shades there, along with the lines of your fingers. That was simple to do, right? This was you being mindful of your palm in the present moment. But think next about bringing mindfulness such as that to your deep sorrows and grief. Think about what it might feel like to call attention to the pain you are feeling. You would likely find this a lot more difficult than paying attention to your palm. This is the difference between simple and difficult mindfulness. Let's start with something easy.

Mindfulness Method Number One: Start by Being Mindful of...

Physical Sensations: How do your hands feel throughout the day? What about your legs or chest? Tap into the sensation of your natural body heat or the way your lungs swell as you breathe.

Walking: How does your foot feel as you walk or run? As you notice the sensation, don't judge or try to change it, but simply observe.

Eating and Drinking: Most of us go through life drinking water and eating food without paying much attention to it. Next time you eat, try noticing every flavor you can sense in the food. Then think about the nourishment it's providing your body with.

Some Words on Mindfulness Meditation:

Meditation is a huge part of learning how to be more mindful since it puts you in touch with the present moment and helps you to back away from your own thoughts. This is perhaps the most classic and well-known method for increasing your awareness in life. In the next chapter, we will go into depth on this along with specific instruction, but this section will serve as a short introduction to meditation.

Shorter Sessions at First: Traditionally, when one learns to meditate through religious means, they have to sit for about an hour. That might work for professionals, but as a beginner, start out smaller than that. In fact, studies show that you can benefit even from short, brief practices in mindfulness. We will get deeper into the meditation aspect of mindfulness later, but for now, keep in mind that starting out with brief sessions is best.

Linking an Enjoyable Activity: There is not one magic amount of time that you should start with for meditation. Rather, you should begin with a number that you are willing to do each and every day. Starting small, such as two to five minutes each day, will help you remember to do it. It also helps to link the activity with something you enjoy. For example, in the morning, you could make a rule that you can't have your morning caffeine until after you have sat in meditation for at least five minutes. Consistency is key to this.

Mindfulness Method Number Two: Find Your Own Personal Motivation.

This is important. Mindfulness is a personal journey; perhaps the most personal one you will ever embark on. This means that you should tailor it to your personality and seek it out where you already have motivation. Perhaps you find it easiest to stay in the present moment when you are with your children. This should be when you decide to practice being mindful of your breath and your surroundings. Although sitting meditation is one method for getting more mindful, it is far from the only way and you must carry this attitude into your daily actions as well if you want it to stick and make a real change for you. Keep in mind that mindfulness is something that you bring to an existing action. Which activity do you most want to bring mindfulness to? Your morning walks? Cooking dinner at night? Or perhaps your breathing as you enjoy nature. Find what you already love and bring mindfulness there.

Worth It and Simple, but Not Always Easy:

As you can tell by reading this far, mindfulness has only great advantages to offer you. But these benefits require hard work and effort, because one has to commit to practicing and meditating daily, even when one would not like to. Sitting with your current experience and present thoughts, even if you do not want to, takes a lot of courage and discipline. We often stifle these feelings and instead get distracted by talking to others, eating when we are not hungry, or going on the internet. You must develop self-discipline if you want to get in touch with direct experience, and this involves sticking with your practice even when you do not yet see the benefits.

Chapter 8: The Air You Breath

When trying to learn how to live life mindfully, the very first thing we can start being more aware of is how we breathe. In particular, deep breathing can help us become more mindful and win over anxiety, and even depression.

Studies on mindfulness breathing also referred to as meditative or deep breathing, have shown that mindfulness breathing could greatly improve our ability to relax and in the process improve our physical and mental health. Meditative breathing can be a very powerful way to refocus our minds on the present without judging it is either wrong or right. By doing this, we can activate our natural relaxation responses that can prove to be very beneficial when it comes to winning against anxiety, stress, and depression.

So, why is meditative breathing or mindfulness of breathing a key aspect in winning the war against are stressors and depression? This is because this method of breathing helps us keep our nervous system from producing more of our stress hormones and instead, turn on that part of the system that is responsible or stopping the pumping of said hormones into our circulatory or blood system. These parts of the nervous system are called the sympathetic and the parasympathetic nervous systems, respectively. This helps our bodies to turn on their relaxation responses that can help slow down our heart rate as well as reduce our blood pressure every time you feel anxious or stressed. The obvious result is calmness.

To achieve these, our brains have to function optimally. And for that to happen, adequate amounts of oxygen are required. It's for this reason that breathing mindfully is crucial to achieve peak mental health – winning the fight against depression, anxiety and stress – and cognitive performance.

Exercises For Mindful Breathing

At this point you may be wondering how we can breathe mindfully? The best way to help you understand how to do it is through this very practical exercise.

Commit 2 minutes daily for practicing mindfulness breathing because if you don't, say goodbye to your chances of successfully learning it.

Choose your sacred space and time of the day to practice mindfulness breathing. Choose the optimal place and time wherein people can't distract or disturb you. It has to be both quiet and comfortable, preferably with a good and comfy chair.

Sit straight on your comfy chair and as you do so, place both your hands on your lap with palms – facing up and open – or down at the side of your body.

Close your eyes and put on a half-smile, which is crucial for this mindful breathing exercise.

Breathe in deeply using your nose. Ensure that your breathe using your diaphragm or tummy instead of your chest. You'll know if you're breathing using your diaphragm if it's your tummy that expands as you breathe in instead of your chest puffing up.

After holding your breath for at least one second, breathe the air out through your mouth while maintaining the half smile mentioned earlier. Wait for at least one second after you've breathed out all the air before repeating several times more.

While you're doing this exercise, don't be surprised to find your mind wandering at first – it's normal. But when this happens, just accept the fact that random thoughts do pop up and acknowledge such thoughts. Don't "kill" such thoughts or "suppress" them but simply let them go or drift away much like smoke being blown away by the wind into the horizon. When the thoughts have already dissipated, re-focus your attention to your breathing. The key is to be aware of or refocus on your breathing whenever random thoughts pop up. Over time, this gets easier.

Once you're done taking deep diaphragm breaths for a few minutes, you can start opening your eyes. If for some reason you feel dizzy, just wait for the feeling to subside before standing up again. Don't be alarmed when this happens though. It's probably because of the significant reduction in your blood pressure as a result of becoming so relaxed with mindful breathing.

As to frequency, there's really no hard and fast rule. What's important is it's practiced at least once daily. And for how long? Again, no hard and fast rule but a good guideline if you're a beginner is 2 minutes tops. Simply increase the duration to 5, 10, or even 30 minutes as you become better at it.

Chapter 9: Preparation To Meditation: Cultivating Attitudes For Mindfulness

Learning mindfulness necessitates that you put your entire self into the process. It is therefore important that you have the right attitude towards this practice. Your attitude is the soil where you will cultivate your capacity to concentrate, calm your mind, see more clearly, and relax your body. Seven interconnected pillars of mindfulness help you naturally enhance this practice. They are as follows:

Beginner's mind

Patience

Determination

Non-striving

Self trust

Non-attachment

Acceptance

Having a **Beginner's Mind** means looking at any situation, no matter how familiar they are, as a whole new experience. It is looking at something as predictable as the sunrise, a breakfast cereal, the road going to work, or your daily meditation with fresh eyes every single day.

Patience is considered as a form of wisdom. It means being completely open to every moment, accepting its fullness, and understanding that things can only unfold in their own time. When you are bored or distracted while meditating, have patience as you allow your mind to eventually reach its desired state.

Determination is important here as well. When you are determined, you stick to the practice; you keep on going even when dark times come or every time you feel there seems little benefit flowing from it. You may hear teachers say, "You do not have to like it, just do it."

On the opposite end, being **non-striving** also plays an important role, particularly in the early days of a practice, when you seem to try too hard to make results. You can strive to lessen your thoughts, to feel the right way, to feel less anxious or depressed, or feel more relaxed. Setting up goals in a wanting or wishing way is simply counterproductive. When you are striving in a mindfulness practice, all you have to do is be aware of what is happening in your body (e.g. focus on a sensation) and return back to meditation.

As a result of all the above attitudes, you cultivate **self-trust** and the ability to let go and accept things as they are. It is about growing faith in your intuition or basic wisdom, and honoring your feelings and innate goodness.

Non-attachment is fundamental to mindfulness. Let go of the thought of how a friend treated you in the past, the fear of a future confrontation, the anticipated pleasure of a vacation. Similarly, let go of each breath and welcome the next one. Let go of any expectations of how your meditation will turn out today—if you will do well or badly or how you will feel at the end. With mindfulness, you learn how to deal with these experiences.

If you choose to let go, you arrive at **acceptance**. However, this does not mean accepting and not doing anything for a current unfavorable condition. It means accepting the truths of the present moment as it is. If you are lost in the streets, what you can do best is accept that truth first instead of rushing in all directions without a clear plan. Afterwards you can place your focus on getting out. Similarly, if you are too distracted during practice, acknowledge it first so you can begin doing appropriate measures to reestablish your meditation.

Chapter 10: Mastering Your Thoughts

After understanding the basics of what mindfulness is and experienced some exercises for yourself, let's look at how you can use mindfulness to shape your inner and outer worlds in more depth.

In this chapter, we'll discuss different ways your mind gets 'stuck,' and the tricks it can play on you. We will discuss using the mindfulness exercises to challenge this, and lead you into a calmer state of being.

What is Anxiety?

Anxiety is a normal part of everyday life. It forms part of our stress-response and helps us to react to situations we deem dangerous. However, for some people this ordinary reaction becomes chronic, leading to heightened senses of threat where there are none.

When people experience anxiety as a chronic state it can have a significantly negative impact on almost every area of daily life.

The heightened states of anxiety we experience are connected with our "fight or flight" response. This response is extremely complex, and can result in significant changes to the nervous system and brain signals.

Anxiety is not only a complex response, but also immediate. We have a strong stress-response that gives us bursts of energy and quick reaction times when under threat. This is understandable when we consider that these systems evolved to help us respond quickly to life-threatening situations in prehistoric times. Viewed in this light, our anxiety is a positive thing. What's less positive is the state we can find ourselves in when anxiety becomes chronic and impedes ordinary functioning.

How Do You Overcome Anxiety?

To tackle anxiety and deal with it effectively, we need to approach it with curiosity, as well as pursuing exercises and ways of thinking and perceiving that will help us to calm our automatic responses.

It helps enormously if you can re-form your ideas about anxiety and not think of is as your enemy. It originally developed as a system that attempts to keep you safe. In this way, viewing anxiety as a well-meaning but misguided friend can be a useful attitude to cultivate. Fighting yourself only leads to an increase in symptoms. So, you need to challenge your anxiety, at the same time as being able to accept it.

You can do this in several ways:

1. Ask Yourself "Is it True?"

One way you can explore anxiety in a positive way is to gently challenge yourself on whether your perceptions and feelings are actually true in your situation. People often get stuck in a way of thinking called 'catastrophizing'. This is a form of thinking where you not only predict the future, but also vividly experience the worst possible result of that potential future.

For example, you might worry about losing your job. For someone with anxiety, it is a short leap from this to believing you will be left with no money, no home, a relationship breakdown and the inability to ever find employment again. Even though part of your mind is aware that this may not be the only outcome, your body and emotional response stick tightly to the worst-case scenario. You then react with fear and panic and the "fight or flight" response kicks in.

Your emotional response is dread, anxiety and fear. However, the truth of your situation is highly unlikely to match the emotional response.

It is important not to begin to judge yourself when you feel this response happening.

Judging yourself negatively for fear-states only compounds them. Instead, try to gently remind yourself of the truth of your situation.

In the above scenario, when the panic response is happening, remember that you are not homeless, jobless or unemployable. Guiding yourself into the present-moment with mindfulness helps you to understand the difference between your emotions and the truth of your situation.

Exercise: When you find yourself overwhelmed by fears you know aren't true, try the partial or full body scan to bring you back into what is really happening in your body. Then, gently challenge yourself on whether the thoughts you had were true or not.

2. The Practice of Presence

There is Buddhist a parable that gives some insight into looking at the world from a present-moment point of view. It's called 'The Tiger and the Strawberry.'

"A man walked through the wilderness, when suddenly he came across a Tiger. The Tiger snarled at him and gave chase, causing the man to flee. He ran and soon came to the edge of a high cliff. The tiger continued to chase him, so in desperation the man climbed down a vine that dangled over the edge of the cliff. He looked below to see another Tiger at the bottom of the deadly drop, and could hear the first tiger snarling above him. Then two mice appeared from a small hole in the cliff next to the vine and began nibbling on it. The man suddenly saw that on the vine were two ripe strawberries. He plucked one and said -"how sweet this strawberry tastes!"

There can be many lessons to take from this parable, but it is an illustration of how being completely in the present moment, a person can experience profound joy, even when past events are negative. The Tigers represent fear and suffering from what has just happened and what will come. The mice gnawing on the vine represent our lack of control, even when we cling to possible solutions. Some people have also suggested that the vine itself can be interpreted as attachment and clinging.

The story is a parable and metaphor for mindfulness. Anxiety tends to be our fierce tigers. Because we cannot escape the stresses and strains of ordinary life, the tigers will always be there. Only by coming into the present moment can we hope to find peace from our past and possible future.

Exercise: Remember the parable when you are catastrophizing. Use the exercise in breathing into your anxiety to lessen the effects of predicting the future or ruminating on the past. If this is too intense, try a partial body scan or standing yoga.

3. Fight your "Monkey Mind"

'Monkey mind' is a way of describing what happens when your mind goes into 'loop' mode. You might be unable to sleep and feel the same thought playing on repeat over and over. Or you might be replaying the same situation from earlier on in the day, unable to stop it.

We all need to reflect on events in our lives. When we have made a mistake, we need to be aware of it and deal with it. By doing this, we are able to plan our short and long-term schedules. However, when this thinking becomes obsessive "Monkey Mind" it stops being helpful and starts to become harmful.

How do you stop monkey mind? As scary as it seems, allowing yourself to really feel and explore the anxiety which is causing the loop is the first step. This isn't about going over and over the same thought. Rather, it is about feeling where the thought is, what its saying and recognizing what's happening. You can also remind yourself about the truth vs. our emotions when tackling 'monkey mind'.

You need to approach this, as much as possible, with a mindset of acceptance and curiosity. One way to really change the nature of the thought is to stop fighting it. You can do a body scan to examine where the thought is being expressed physically. Is your stomach tight? Are your hands shaking? Are you breathing differently? How does it feel?

By taking this approach you begin to befriend the sensation with a sense of curiosity.

The next step is to take it as lightheartedly as possible. It sounds difficult, but cultivating an attitude of "Oh there goes Monkey Brain again!!" takes the power out of it, while still acknowledging it. This is a skill that can take a little time to learn, but once you begin to see these thoughts in a curious, lighthearted way, they begin to pass more freely.

Exercise: Monkey Mind often happens at nighttime when we are trying to sleep. Get out of bed and do a short Standing Yoga exercise. Stretching your muscles and coming back into your body helps to challenge that loop. You may also practice a full body scan.

Chapter 11: Formal Mindfulness Meditation

There are two ways to develop mindfulness - formal and informal. In formal practice, you are setting aside a time and place to practice mindfulness, while an informal practice means becoming mindful in everyday life.

This chapter delves into these two practices, along with tips and clear guides on how to fall into a meditative state.

Formal Mindfulness Meditation

To start off your path to mindfulness, you have to cultivate a formal practice first. Ten to twenty minutes of formal meditation will open you up to become more mindful in everyday life.

A few tips before you start:

Wear something comfy. Make sure your clothes are just right and don't distract you from your meditation.

Don't start meditating with a full stomach or when you're hungry. Hunger can distract you from meditation, while being too full can make you feel drowsy. The best time will be 1 hour after a meal or 15 minutes after a light snack.

Find a comfortable place and time where you won't be disturbed. If you have a busy schedule, right after waking up and before going to bed is great. Make sure to privacy so that you won't feel self-conscious as you practice.

Mindful Eating Meditation

This meditation is simple and easy to do, giving you a positive ground to work from when you try other mindfulness exercises.

Use a piece of fruit for this, such as a strawberry or a grape, but other food items that you can hold in your hand is okay as well, such as hard candy or dry bread. A grape will be used as an example in the guide.

Step 1: Take the piece of grape in your hand. Look at it with fresh eye. Note the color, shape and firmness of the grape. Note how the light is reflected on its skin.

Step 2: Smell the grape. Note the scent it gives off, as well as the physical reactions you feel.

Step 3: Now close your eyes and feel the grape in your hand. Note the texture in your fingers. Feel the shape and the weight of the grape. Squeeze the grape gently between your fingers. Smell the grape again.

Step 4: Finally, bring the grape to your lips. Gently put it into your mouth and roll it around your mouth. Softly put a bit of pressure on the grape and note the taste of the juice in your tongue. Now place it between your teeth and, as slowly as possible, bite into it. Chew as slowly as possible and note the sensations that this brings. Note the aftertaste.

After completing this mindful eating meditation exercise, try to answer the following questions honestly:

How was the experience for you?

Did the meditative exercise help you experience eating the grape in a new way?

Do you think this will change how you appreciate eating grapes from now on?

Please keep in mind that every experience differs and that there is no right and wrong way of going about these meditative exercises. Don't worry about getting right and discovering something profound. Simply be aware and lose yourself in the experience.

Mindful Breathing

Mindful breathing meditation is one of the most basic meditation techniques out there, and it's one you can do within ten minutes. This meditation technique helps you focus your awareness on your breath. This technique also gives you space to practice guiding your thoughts back to your breath whenever your mind wanders.

Step 1: Sit or lie down in a comfortable position. You can sit on a chair, or sit cross legged on the floor, or you can even lie down on the floor if you want. It doesn't really matter what posture you choose as long as you are comfortable. Just make sure you don't fall asleep if you happen to be lying down. Try to keep your spine as straight as possible.

This part is all about you. There is nothing you need to perfect or achieve right now. You simply need to be aware of being. You don't need to do anything. Simply be aware of each moment as it passes and relax your body. Close your eyes if you feel like it.

Step 2: Focus your awareness on your breath. Feel the air going in and out of your mouth or nose. Be aware of the rise and fall of your chest. Listen to the sounds of your own breathing.

At some point during this 10-minute exercise, random thoughts may pop up. Don't panic or get worried, and don't blame yourself. Simply acknowledge the thought or emotion and let it go. Be at peace with everything that pops into your brain then move on. Gently direct your attention back to your breathing and focus on your breath.

Step 3: Continue this meditation for 10 minutes without altering the depth or quickness of your breath. When you are ready, gently open your eyes.

Mindful Movement Meditation

Mindful movement, through slow and deliberate stretches and poses, is a great way to prepare yourself physically and mentally for longer meditations. If mindful movement is done with full awareness, it can be one of the most immersive formal meditation techniques out there.

A good example of mindful movement will be yoga techniques. Yoga requires all of your concentration and awareness of breath, but you can also do mindful movement meditation with simple and standard stretches.

Here are some pointers when it comes to practicing mindful movement:

Test your limits. There is often a limit to your flexibility and range of motion, and reaching or pushing beyond these limits can cause a lot of pain and discomfort. Mindful movement gives an opportunity to explore your own reactions as you reach these limits.

You become more open, receptive and even familiar with physical discomfort. The sensation and pain does not change, but your reaction and tolerance of it does.

Get in tune with your body. When you focus on the sensations and feeling you have as you do your poses, you become aware of the present and start to live in the moment. You are present in your body and you are aware of every moment passing rather than experiencing the present through a haze of wandering thoughts.

Prepares you for informal meditation. With mindful meditation, you are learning to move your body while in a meditative state, an essential skill if you want to start informal meditation in daily life. With more practice, you can take walks, cook and even run errands in full mindfulness.

Think of the lessons you can learn through mindful movement. Take into consideration, for example, the fluidity of movement needed for you to stay balanced, how your body is not stiff or still, but always correcting itself to hold difficult poses. This is how life is as well.

You cannot be unchanging and unmovable. You must be fluid. No matter how many things change around you, or how many bumps you encounter along the way, you can still stay in balance by shifting your position slightly.

The Body Scan Technique

This technique should take at least half an hour and is one of the most extensive meditation techniques you will learn. It is important to feel comfortable, secure and at ease as you do this, so remember to choose a place and time that is conducive to your relaxation. It would be a good idea to give the people you live with a heads up about your practice so that they can consciously try not to disturb you.

Remember that this technique is all about focusing awareness on your body as it is. There is no right or wrong way to do this. All you need is to simply be.

Although this technique is safe, it may bring some buried emotions to the surface. If you feel like you can't cope with this resurgence of feeling anymore, then stop. Try to ask for advice from a therapist or mindfulness guide if you feel at a loss, but keep in mind that allowing buried emotions to resurface is the first step to healing. The sooner you face and acknowledge these emotions, the sooner you can cope with them.

Step 1: Choose a position that you can hold for half an hour or so. You can sit on a comfortable chair with your hands resting on your lap or you can sit cross-legged on the floor.

You can choose to lie down on a blanket or yoga mat with your arms to your side, legs hip width apart and your palms facing up. Do everything you can to be comfortable. You can use a pillow under your knees or rest your head on, as long as you are comfy. You can place a light blanket over your body as it may get cold when you lay still for a long while.

Step 2: After choosing a comfortable position, start to feel the weight of your own body as you bring your awareness to your breath. Focus your attention on the places where your body is in contact with the chair, floor or mat. Continue to breathe evenly. You can choose to close your eyes for better focus.

Step 3: As you breathe, allow your body to sink deeper into the chair, mat or against the floor. Bring your awareness to your breath. Feel the air going in and out of your mouth and nose. Feel the rise and fall of your belly and chest. Do this until you feel your body becoming more relaxed.

Step 4: When you feel fully into the meditation, start to direct your attention down toward your left leg, down below your ankle and foot. Direct your focus toward the big toe of your left foot. Note all of the sensations that arise from your big toe with a beginner's mind. Treat the experience as if it's a new one, filled with curiosity and wonder. Is your toe hot or cold? What sensations do you feel? If you can't feel anything, simply be aware of the lack of sensation.

Step 5: Start to expand your awareness toward your other toes, then your whole foot, all the while maintaining focus awareness. Continue to measure your breath.

Step 6: Imagine your breath going in and coursing into your body as you inhale. Visualize your breath going back out the way it came as you exhale. Visualize this entry and exit of breath in the body part that you are focusing on. Do this for a few minutes.

Step 7: Now, gently direct your focus upwards towards the sole of your foot. Focus on the heel and ball of your foot, then up towards the ankle until your focus is on your left foot as a whole. Continue to breathe into this body part.

Step 8: Once you are ready, direct your awareness upward to your left leg below the knee. Repeat the steps of focused awareness and breathing into your left leg. Once you're ready, let go of your awareness of your left leg. Notice how different your left leg feels compared to your right leg.

Step 9: Continue directing your awareness higher up, toward your hips, pelvis, and buttocks. Then back down toward your right leg. From there, direct your focus upward to your lower abdomen, then your chest. Breathe delicately into your organs. Visualize your breath going in and nourishing your organs.

From your torso, direct your awareness to the fingertips of your left hand, up the arm and down the right arm again. Next comes your neck, jaw, face, forehead and crown. Pay particular attention to the center of your forehead and tip of your skull.

Step 10: After scanning your whole body, expand your attention to its entirety. Visualize the breath sweeping up and down your entire body. Feel the warmth and nourishment that each breath brings with it. Do this for a few more minutes.

Step 11: Now let go of your awareness of your body and feel your mind and body melt together. Be at peace with every aspect of yourself, your body and mind are one. Remember that this sense of oneness is always available and within you.

Step 12: Gently return your focus to the surface slowly and gently. Open your eyes slowly and reflect on your experience. Work on bringing your mindful awareness to whatever task you need to do next.

These formal meditation techniques will be the first stepping stones in your journey towards living mindfully. Keeping up a regular practice can be a great help on your path to living in the moment.

Chapter 12: Start With Relaxation And Breathing

Once you've read this book and decided to commit to practicing mindfulness, you can begin your first session. The first step is to get into as relaxed a state as possible. Then, you can enter into mindfulness by focusing on your breath.

Prepare to Be Mindful

The first few times you begin a mindfulness session, you need to put some thought into preparing for it. This involves paying attention to practical details. You need to choose where to be mindful and what you're going to do as you get into the mindful mode.

Later on, you'll develop the skills to be mindful in any situation and in any place. For now, though, choose a quiet place with only a few distractions. You might find it helpful to set an alarm on your smartphone or use a kitchen timer for the amount of time you intend to stay in a mindful state. This allows you to stop paying attention to how much time has passed and maintain your focus on the present time, moment by moment.

It's usually best to start with a seated mindfulness meditation so you can concentrate better. So, choose a place and a seat and get together anything you need, such as pillows or a yoga mat.

Get Comfortable

You need to take care of your physical needs before you start with your first mindfulness sessions. If you don't, your session is going to be disrupted when you re-situate your body or shiver from the cold. As you develop your mindfulness skills, you can allow these distractions, knowing that are a part of your life experience. However, right now, make sure the temperature of the room isn't too hot or cold for you. If you want to practice mindfulness in an outdoor setting, that's okay as long as the temperature isn't extreme. Make sure you're in a position in which you won't get any cramps, numbness or pain you can avoid. Again, being mindful in difficult situations will come later. For now, keep the temperature mild and get comfortable using pillows or blankets.

Do Relaxation Exercises

Learning to relax can be a major hurdle to being mindful. You can fly over that roadblock as easily as an experienced track runner if you use specific exercises to do it. It can be helpful to do a systematic muscle relaxation exercise.

In your seated or reclined position, think about your toes and tighten those muscles as hard as you can. Keep them tight for 10 seconds, counting off each second in your mind or out loud. Then, release the muscles of your toes all at once. Imagine that your toes are floppy and boneless. Next, move up to your feet and tighten and relax them in the same way. Keep moving up your body, one muscle group at a time, until you're relaxing the muscles in your face and head.

Another relaxation exercise is to picture a calming scene. For instance, you can imagine you're sitting beside a slow-moving river. Then, imagine leaves floating downstream lazily. When thoughts or worries arise, imagine putting them on a leaf and letting them continue their journey down the river without you.

Focus on Your Breath

You're always breathing, obviously. You have to be to be alive. However, how often do you pay attention to your breath? If you're like most people, you only notice your breathing when there's something wrong with it. You might be doing a strenuous activity and finding it hard to breathe normally. Or, you might have a cold and it takes a greater than usual effort to breathe as deeply as you usually do. During your mindfulness session, you need to stay more focused on your breath.

Try breathing in slowly, to a count of 8. Hold the breath for 4 to 8 counts, and then release it gradually to another count of 8. When you've exhaled fully, wait for another count of 4 to 8 before moving on to the next inhale. Imagine that your breath is coming and going in a circular pattern.

Another technique is to imagine something positive coming in with each inhale and something negative being released with each exhale. For instance, you might think of peacefulness coming in with each inhale and stress going out with each exhale. Whenever your mind wanders to the past or future, go back to focusing on your breath. Don't expect yourself to be perfect. Instead, release those negative judgments and keep going back to your breath focus.

Settle into a Steady Breathing Pattern

Once you're completely relaxed and focused on your breath, you can let your breathing settle in to a gentle and rhythmic pattern. At that point, you're fully prepared to experience the moment mindfully. You can begin to notice what's happening around you and let your breath take care of itself in the relaxed way you've developed in the preceding moments.

Come Back to Your Breath As Needed

With the previous preparation completed, your breathing should take care of itself, at least for a while. You'll shift your focus to the world outside you and to your personal feelings and bodily sensations. However, any time you lose that focus, you can always come back to your breath and start again.

Chapter 13: Anxiety

There are many misconceptions when it comes to what an anxiety disorder is. People need to realize that it is more than just being nervous or edgy. A person who suffers from anxiety attacks will have unrealistic exaggeration of different threats. They can also become suspicious and enter into a repetitive cycle of negative thinking. Imagine feeling an amplified form of fear, which then kicks your fight or flight response into overdrive. This can significantly hinder you from doing what you need to do, disrupt your focus and in some cases, even affect you physically.

So how do you counter this and prevent it from happening? Be mindful and remain present in your body. By being aware of your body and self in this moment, you can respond rationally and positively to any threats instead of immediately going into the fight or flight mode.

Here are some exercises to try:

Count your breathing.

Starting to feel anxious? Close your eyes and take a couple of deep breaths. After this, start counting backwards from 20 to 1. Make sure that you keep breathing evenly while you do this and that you do not rush through the process. Take as much time as you need, it's not about speed. Instead, the goal is to get your mind into a more relaxed state. Repeat this as many times as you need.

Some people like doing this practice while walking so if you have some space available, try it out. Getting up and doing something will be helpful when it comes to putting yourself at ease.

Scribbling.

Carry a notebook with you and a pen to write with. Anytime you start feeling anxious, write down what you're feeling and try to observe these sensations without getting too attached to them. Write things down as if you were watching them happen from another perspective. If you find that you can't yet focus and the anxiety is still increasing, try doodling or scribbling randomly. You can also draw if you want to. This should help your mind focus on one thing and shift your thoughts away from the ones that are causing your negativity.

Move around.

Get up from where you are and go for a walk. Focus your mind on counting your every step. You need not go far or to somewhere specific when you do this. It could be as simple as walking up and down some stairs or get yourself something to drink. The most important aspect of this exercise is your focus. Take time with every step and be in that moment. 5 minutes may not seem like much, but if you're being mindful within that timeframe, it could mean the difference between a panic attack and a calm mind.

Focus on a mantra.

This could be anything that motivates and empowers you, something that will remind you that you have power over your thoughts and how you choose to react to them. Have this mantra anywhere that's visible. It could be on your work desk or the area where you do most of your tasks. Anytime you feel anxious, turn to this mantra and focus on it. Think about why it makes you feel good and allow that feeling to fill you up. It does not need to be a single mantra, too! If you have a few that give you positive feelings, always make sure you have them visible.

Acknowledge the feeling then let it go.

Fighting against your anxiety will be futile and getting angry at yourself for not being able to be "better" at it or for not being "normal" will only make you feel bad about yourself. Acknowledge the problem and remind yourself that you are doing the best you can for it. It isn't always being aggressive and more often than not, anxiety is best treated in a calm manner. So you had a bad one today. Let the negativity go and focus on doing better next time. Recover today so you can work on everything tomorrow.

Talk to someone you trust.

It would also help if you talk about what you're feeling to someone you're comfortable with. They should be able to help put things in perspective and let you see the things you may not be able to see at the moment. Be present when doing this and make sure you open your mind to their advice. The mere presence of another person can sometimes be the only thing someone with anxiety needs. Offer no judgment to anyone who tries to help and simply be present with them. Let go of your fears and insecurities as you do this.

Dealing with anxiety is no easy task. There will be good days, bad days and ones in which you are completely in the dark. Don't fight it. Be present with what you're feeling and analyse each one. In doing this, you can process everything and realize that things are only bad inside your head. Once you become aware of that, your consciousness will shift to something more positive.

Chapter 14: Simple Forms Of Meditation

When starting meditation you want to use a simple form that you can adjust easily to and that is comfortable for you. You do not have to be sitting cross-legged on the floor in the classic Meditation pose you can sit on a chair if this is more comfortable for you.

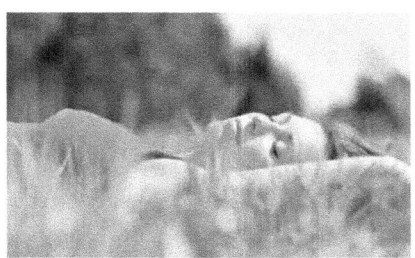

The main thing is that you are in a comfortable position when practising your meditation. Below are two simple forms of meditation. Give each one of them a try to see which form best suits you. Most importantly enjoy the experience!

1) Watching the Breath. This form of meditation is the easiest to follow being that you just need to gently pay attention to your natural flow in your breathing. Just pure attention on your breathing paying a bit more attention to your outer breath. During this meditation do not become fixated or tense. Be lightly aware of your breathing if you get distracted don't worry just gently pull yourself back to paying gentle attention to your breathing but remain spatially.

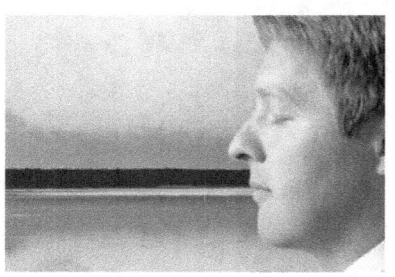

2) Focus on Object. Find an object to sit your focus gently on or resting on. Don't focus too intensely on it just on the outer surface. It can be an object that may have a sacred significance or not. If you find your mind drifting away from the object try and lightly pull it back to the object. If you are distracted by something wait and then go back to focusing on the object. Your mind will eventually become rested. It will rest within itself in a state of non-distraction. This is what meditation is.

Key Points to Remember When Starting Meditation Session.

Posture:

Keep your back straight

hands lightly resting on your knees or in your lap

spread your shoulders

slightly lower chin

mouth open slightly

eyes open gazing slightly downward

Remember to....

keep mind at peace, breathing naturally, sitting comfortably

let thoughts and emotions come and go to not try and hold them

do not do running commentary

rest your attention lightly on your outer breath or an object

if you get distracted just find your way back to your breath or object

don't judge yourself, don't be tense just relax

Be Aware....

mindful of the object or breath

stay open and spacious

aware of being distracted

How Long for Each Session?

I recommend that you should try at least 15 minutes each day. If you prefer to sit longer it is totally up to you. Also that goes for shorter sessions too. If you feel 15 minutes is too long perhaps you can start with 5 minute sessions and build from there. The main thing that is important here is not how long your sessions are but finding a routine that is truly working for you; that is what matters.

Mental Attitude is Important. When you are practising meditation all you need to learn how to do is to let go and relax your mind and body. Allow things that arise to arise but rest, open in the present moment. Once you learn how to remain in this awareness you will realize that you are much larger than your thoughts and emotions and perceptions toward life.

When you discover the confidence of your true nature nothing will make you afraid anymore such as thoughts and emotions. You will become free of them and no longer chained to them. Become aware of thoughts and emotions but do not follow them. Just be aware of them for what they are. By resting our minds in their natural awareness we will be completely unaffected by anything that does arise. Like anything else that you truly want to be successful at it will take time, patience and practice to get the full results that you want to reach.Remember it won't happen in one session you must commit to doing at least one session a day to truly reap the full benefits of meditation. Start with small sessions and build on to them as you further progress in your meditation practices.

Keep a good positive attitude and you will soar lifting your mind out and above the dark clouds that can cloud your mind; meditation will help you to clear the clouds from your mind. In their place you will have a clear mind filled with peace and contentment. You will be filled with "inner riches."

Chapter 15: Mindfulness Meditation

Mindfulness meditation is also known as 'Vipassana', its background is based on Buddhist tradition. It is the most popular form of meditation in the Western world. This form is about being present in the here and now, allowing your mind to run, accepting thoughts and allowing them to come and go while you practise detachment from each thought. It teaches you to be aware of your breathing which is considered to be one of many other sensations not any particular focus on it. There is no attempts using this form of meditation to try and change breathing patterns. When you change your breathing patterns it changes the energy. In this practise it wants you to only observe your breathing patterns. If for example your breathing pattern is shallow this can mean you are stuck in a low-energy state.

Meditation is a way in which many of us use in helping to train our minds not unlike the fitness training we use to train or exercise our bodies in a more physical sense. When using meditation you will learn ways in which you are able to give your brain a workout of sorts that will help to ensure that it is performing at its best. In life there are many things that are beyond our control but when it comes to our minds we must take responsibility for the health of our minds by using an approach such as meditation to help guide us in learning how to make our minds healthier. It is believed in Buddhism that if we can learn to take care of our minds through meditation it will also be the antidote for many conditions that affect us humans such as our personal fears and anxieties that we suffer from. The practice of meditation is like a gateway towards finding inner peace and contentment.

Meditation can Transform your Mind. You can transform your mind through the use of meditation helping you to see your inner self and the world around you in a whole new different light. Using Buddhist meditation it will help to encourage a calm view of your surroundings in the world, giving you clarity, concentration, and will develop your emotional positivity within yourself. Once you begin the practice of certain particular forms of meditation you will become aware of the patterns and habits of your mind. You will find more positive ways to live and cultivate your life through using Meditation. When you begin to use meditation on a regular basis you are going to find that you are able to focus on things better and you will have an overall feeling of energized states of mind and soul that are peaceful. It can lead you to a major transformation in how you look at life in general having a better and more positive outlook through the use of meditation.

Discovering Inner Peace & Contentment. We all want to find total happiness and contentment with no pain or suffering in life. We rush around in life in a constant frenzy trying to find the ultimate form of happiness and contentment on the outside. The world we live in is always filling our heads with things we should have if we really want to be happy. Making us think we must live in a big house, drive a flashy car, have great looks and of course lots of money to be truly happy. These options in finding happiness are not long lasting choices as they never seem to bring people true long lasting happiness and contentment. The constant desire for more and more things is like a terrible addiction that we are never able to truly satisfy we just want more and more. We are putting the world we live at great risk because of our enormous levels of greed we are killing our planet earth (our home) all in the need to fulfil our greedy appetites. We don't stop long enough to really absorb in and understand the terrible damage we are doing worldwide to our environment all in the pursuit of some form of short lived happiness.

Two Kinds of Happiness. There are two basic forms of happiness in life: 1) physical happiness and 2) mental happiness or contentment. The physical is based on our "outer riches" and the mental covers our "inner riches" in life. Many of us spend way too much of our time trying to collect more "outer wealth" that we become totally obsessed with the gathering of more and more "outer wealth" that we no longer have time just to enjoy life's simple pleasures. The outcome of this is little to no time put towards finding "inner riches" such as having compassion towards others.

But if you are able to learn by using meditation on how to focus more on your "inner wealth" you will find that you will be happier in your mind even when you are facing hardships in life. In understanding about "outer wealth" and "inner wealth" it will help you to understand why there is people in the world that seem to have all the "outer wealth" anyone could want but yet they still seem like lost or unhappy souls compared to others that always seem to be happy and content in life even during hardships with little to no "outer wealth." By using meditation as a tool you will be able to find your "inner wealth" which will be a more rewarding and long lasting form of happiness than anything you will experience with "outer wealth."

Key Points When Starting Meditation Session

Posture:

make sure your back is straight

have your hands resting lightly on your knees or your lap

spread your shoulders open

keep your mouth slightly open

slightly lower your chin

have your eyes closed and slightly gazing downward

Also Keep in Mind to:

sit comfortably, breathing naturally, keep mind at peace

do not try to hold emotions or thoughts let them come and go

do not do a verbal running commentary of session

make sure to rest your attention lightly on object or breath

find your way back if you get distracted to what you are focusing on breath/object

just relax and enjoy meditation session do not judge yourself think positive

Including Mindfulness in your Day-to-day Activities.

When you begin using Mindfulness in your daily activities it will help to improve your mental and physical health. Using concentration which is a form of meditation and acceptance, and being able to pay attention to the thoughts and sensations around you. You need to find a method to practice Mindfulness that you feel comfortable with.

Chapter 16: Finding Mindfulness At Work

The combination of increased responsibility and a general decrease in the level of control over one's life makes the workday the most stressful part of the day for most people, and with good reason. This perfect storm of stress naturally leads to increased levels of anxiety and tension, generally without any hope of relief in sight. However, you can flip the script on this daily occurrence by discreetly making mindfulness a part of your daily workplace routine.

Practicing mindfulness in the workplace will not only decrease stress and anxiety, but it can also make it easier for you to focus on a particularly difficult project or help you find the solution to the problem you have been stuck on for weeks. Being mindful at work does this by making it easier for you to think outside the box. While not everyone will be able to take advantage of mindfulness practices at work, with a little bit of practice most people should be able to find some time to squeeze a little bit of mindfulness in between their other tasks.

While, individually, the amount of benefit that each one of these micro-mindfulness exercises provides is minimal the effects are cumulative – which means that the end result will ultimately lead to a sense of inner peace that is greater than the sum of its parts. While it might seem difficult to juggle the demands of the day, the demands of your coworkers and everything else that life throws at you, you can consider each micro mindfulness session as an island of calm in an otherwise choppy sea.

Getting started

Mindfulness in the workplace should be used as a tool for the purpose of squeezing out every last bit of efficiency from the day that you can. Do this by thinking about how you can use your time as productively as possible during each micro mindfulness session. If you are already using your commute to practice mindfulness, then when you arrive at work you will already be in a mindful state that will allow you to get the most out of each moment. In order to keep the mindfulness train rolling, you will want to take a moment or two between tasks in order to focus on your breathing and thus the sensory data that your body is providing.

This doesn't need to be the sort of elaborate process that you learned to complete at home; it should only take a minute or two to ensure your head remains on straight throughout the day. Quantity trumps quality in this situation and if you practice each time you switch tasks you will find that your early-morning mindfulness state persists throughout the day. This is not to say that you fail if you can't take a moment to be mindful between every set of tasks though. As long as you fit in some sessions of mindful thinking whenever and wherever you can you will come out miles ahead in the long-term.

For many people, clearing their mind during the work day can be extremely difficult. If your job leaves you little time to sneak in a bit of mindfulness, simply start with whatever you can get – even if it is just 30 seconds. Over time, you will get a feel for the solace and figure out the best ways to chain dozens, if not hundreds, of mindfulness sessions together throughout the day.

Micro-mindfulness options

Focus on your fingers: If you work an office job, then one of the easiest ways to sneak in a bit of mindfulness is to spend some time focusing on the way your fingers move as they glide across the keyboard. You can focus on the rhythmic sound the keys make as they are pressed, and if you focus hard enough you can pick out the individual sensations of each keypress as it happens. Take some time to consider the way in which your mind forms words before your fingertips tap them out. Consider the connection between the body and the mind that is at play and the ways in which you typically take it all for granted.

Watch your posture: If you spend most of your day in an office chair, then focusing on your posture is another good way to sneak in a bit of mindfulness. You can begin by relaxing your entire body, beginning with your neck and working all the way down to the tips of your toes. After you have relaxed, you will then be able to more clearly focus on the signals being provided by your body in an effort to locate any pain points. Once these points have been identified, you can then adjust your posture until you are completely free of pain and so that you can refocus on the task at hand.

Respond slower: If much of your day consists of responding to the requests of others, either via email or over the phone, then a great way to throw in some extra mindfulness is to simply take 30 seconds between each request to re-center yourself and practice being mindful in a microburst. This has the added benefit of helping you clear your mental state before conversing with others. While 30 seconds might not seem like much, it can actually add up quite quickly. For example, if you deal with 70 requests that require your response per day you are actually spending 35 minutes of your day being mindful. Give it a try; you will be surprised at how much extra mindfulness you can sneak in on an average day.

Look for opportunities for repetition: Any scenario that requires routine or repetition is always a great opportunity for practicing mindfulness. The best activities are those that combine basic physical activity with the freedom to focus exclusively on the task at hand as they are essentially a free pass to practice mindfulness. To do so successfully, all you need to do is focus on the task to the exclusion of all else, and you should be able to easily fill your head with mindful thoughts.

Focus on your coworkers: If your days are spent constantly interacting with your coworkers, then you can find an opportunity to be mindful by devoting all of your mental focus to listening to whatever it is that they have to say. While this is not to say that the insights from your coworkers are all going to be winners or optimistic, but focusing the full scope of your attention on them can allow you to find a state of mindfulness that will also make them feel as though you are really committed to hearing them out.

Prepare for your end of the day commute: In order to maximize the effectiveness of your time spent being mindful on your commute home, you should try and use the last few minutes of your workday to wrap things up as much as possible and then compartmentalize everything so that nothing follows you home. Take some time to think about all of the things you have already accomplished, reflect on your various failures and successes, and how they fit into the big picture. Once you have finished reflecting, mentally close the door on the workday with the understanding that any leftover problems don't need to be solved until tomorrow. You will find that doing so makes your evening mindfulness session even more effective than it might otherwise be. Above all, repeat the mantra that tomorrow is another day and another opportunity to get everything right.

Notice the benefits of mindfulness at work: While you may feel that taking the time out of your day to be mindful at work causes you to work more slowly, the reality is that the opposite is true. In fact, the more hectic your job is the more you likely spend time reacting to things without thinking them through fully. Once you start being more mindful, however, you will find that your mind is clear enough to stop reacting to things in the moment and is instead able to proactively respond to situations in a productive manner.

With enough time spent practicing mindfulness at work, you will likely find it easier to come up with new approaches to problems both new and old. This is only going to be the case, however, if you stop thinking about the situations you find yourself in as problems and start thinking about them as challenges to be overcome. Problems are simply roadblocks to success while challenges, on the other hand, are incidents that can be learned from and bested for the betterment of you and your place of business. When you come across a challenge that has you stumped, consider writing it down and focusing on it completely to the exclusion of everything else. If you have been practicing mindfulness regularly you will be surprised at how quickly a previously unthought-of solution may reveal itself.

7 Minutes Mindful Breathing Meditation

Practicing this 7-minutes mindful breathing meditation twice daily will help you become more mindful and stay focused with an overall greater sense of calmness and clarity over time.

It helps to think of this exercise as a mental exercise that helps strengthen your attention muscles by directing your awareness inwards and challenging yourself to stay focused.

According to a recent mindfulness study, some Harvard researchers found that daily practice of this mindful technique for 8 weeks helped increase the sense of clarity and peace in the meditators as compared to non-meditators. Their MRIs also showed a visible increase in the gray matter present in some important parts of the brain.

Let us learn how to do this breathing exercise:

1. Sit comfortably with your spine straightened and breathe slowly and evenly

2. Count your in breaths and out breaths from 1-10. Count one inhale and one exhale until you get to 10. Repeat when you count to 10.

3. Repeat the cycle five consecutive times.

4. Once you have completed the 5 cycles of counting your in breaths and out breaths,

continue breathing at this calm, steady pace for about 2-3 minutes.

5.Visualize your breath moving through your respiratory system and appreciate the physical relationship between your breaths and your body. The whole exercise should last for 7 minutes.

To enhance your mindfulness, add the 5 minutes body scan to your daily mindfulness. Let us learn more about this in the following chapter.

5 Minutes Body Scan Meditation

This meditation technique is ideal for building body awareness and increasing your mindfulness. It is also a great tool for easing off tension at the end of your day and helps you sleep better at night.

The 5 minutes body scan meditation allows you to identify where stress resides in your body and helps you release it with your increased awareness and relax more. Including this body scan meditation in your list of mindfulness practices helps reduce sleep problems very significantly according to a research report.

What to do:

1.Sit or lay down comfortably.

2.Take a few moments to keep your breaths calm and steady.

3.Bring your whole awareness to your bodily sensations.

4.Spend a number of slow breaths on different focal points in your body.

5.Begin with your left toes, your left foot, left ankle, left calf, left knee, left thigh and work your way up to your left hip.

6.Breathe into any area of discomfort or tension you find and repeat on the out breath.

7.Repeat this through your right side and follow through with your pelvic region, abdomen and lower back.

8.Move up to your torso and back region and from there follow and breathe through every single sensation in your fingers, hands, wrists, arms, shoulders, your neck, jaw, your temples, ears, eyes, your forehead, your crown and your entire head right to your skull.

The following chapters will focus on other mindful techniques that you can adopt.

Mindful Observation

Mindful observation is an amazing technique that helps you to notice and appreciate those simple and easily ignored elements you find in your life and environment more profoundly. The aim of this mindfulness exercise is to help you connect with the beauty of your natural environment-things you have always missed as you run around hastily to meet your daily goals. The more you practice mindful observation, the more you become more mindful of things and the more you learn to take note of things in the moment.

How to practice mindful observation:

1.Choose any object of your choice in your natural environment and focus on it for 2-3 minutes. This object could be anything like a beautiful flower, an insect, a plant, the moon or clouds.

2.Make sure you do nothing other than noticing the object you are focusing on. Simply relax and watch the object for as long as you can concentrate on it.

3.Focus on this object and observe it like you have never seen it before.

4.Visually explore all aspects of the object's formation, allow yourself to be thoroughly consumed by its presence, beauty and nature.

5.Allow yourself to become connected with the energy of that object and all of its purpose in that natural environment.

From mindful observation, you can get right into mindful awareness to help you further increase your level of mindfulness:

Mindful Awareness

This exercise is designed mainly to help you cultivate an increased level of awareness and appreciation of your day-to-day simple tasks and chores and all the results they help you achieve and how they work in synergy to make your life exciting and more successful. As you practice mindful awareness, it becomes easier to concentrate on tasks you are working on and you end up doing them even better.

Let us now learn how to practice mindful awareness:

1. Think of anything you know that happens two or more times every day; something you have always taken for granted and overlooked, such as opening the door, turning on the water tap, turning on the heater or any other home electronic appliance.

2. If for instance you thought about opening the door, pay more attention to the processes involved from unlocking the door, to turning the doorknob, to opening the door. Be mindful of where you are at that moment, what you are doing, why you are doing it, etc. Notice how you feel while opening the door and think about where the door leads. Appreciate the

hands that turn the doorknob, the legs that walk through the door and the brain that coordinates all of these functions. Do the same when you open your computer to start your daily work, turn the car's ignition, etc.

3.If you notice any negative thoughts while doing any of these things mindfully, such as, remembering you are opening the door to go settle a dispute, see your doctor, answer a query at work, write a difficult exam, etc, take some time to release all the negativities, fears and worries. Once you do that, fill your mind with appreciation for the job, the opportunity to be in school, the good health you have enjoyed thus far and any positive side of what you are presently facing or going to face.

Chapter 17: Spirituality

Contrary to what a lot of people think, this has very little to do with religion. It's all about feeling at one with the universe. Let me try to explain this in simple terms. Sometimes, you are so awed by nature that you stop in your tracks and feel this feeling inside you that can't be described. Sometimes a particularly poignant piece of music can do the same thing. It awakens something inside you that you didn't know was there. This is your spiritual connection to the world around you. As children, we are very aware of our surroundings, but life tends to stifle that. Ask a child what he sees on a cold and frosty morning and he's likely to tell you he sees the magic of snowflakes on the window whereas a grown up sees the dark side of everything and merely sees the morning as presenting another cold day. When you see and enjoy the spiritual side of mindfulness, you become more aware and can see beyond the negative toward those things in life that you may have seen as a child.

Can you ever remember having looked at the face of a baby and seeing that look of sheer wonder in the baby's eyes? The baby notices changes in light. It notices colors. The baby also notices sounds, scents, noises. That's because the baby has not yet reached the age where other input gets into the way of the way the child perceives the world. Unfortunately, all of that wonder is bashed out of us over the years by what is summed up as reality. In fact, it doesn't have to be your reality. When you step into the spiritual side of mindfulness, you will suddenly notice that the seasons of your life are colored with so much detail that you may not have noticed for a long time.

Take a spiritual journey

I want you to take a spiritual journey with me and go to visit a place that you find fills you with awe. This differs from person to person. To one, it may be sunrise on a beach. To another, it may be sunset on a hill. Yet another may find that awe inspiring thought process in the garden early in the morning when the cobwebs that have been formed overnight are spilling over with dew drops that make them look like wonderful beaded necklaces. You are the only person who can make that choice for you.

What I want you to do when you are in that place is to find a place to sit and simply breathe in the way that I showed you earlier. Keep your eyes open this time because while you breathe, I want you to look around you and absorb that scene that inspires you. This was a journey that I took many years ago while going through mindfulness training. What I found was that everything around me reminded me of how small I was in comparison with the wonders of the world. You may wonder why someone may want to look small, but it isn't hard to understand once you have experienced it. No matter how small you are, you feel that you are closer to your creator – whoever that may be – and that it's not a question of your stature. It's a question of your understanding of your own significance. If there were no grains of sand on the beach, there would not be a beach. Thus, in this kind of ambiance, you are able to drop all of your doubts about yourself and simply accept yourself for who you are.

Take in all of the elements around you using all of your senses. See the colors, feel the wind against your skin or the warmth of the sun. Touch the air around you and feel the thrill of being in such an inspiring place. It helps you to put things back into perspective and that's a wonderful thing to do when you seem to be going through too many bleak winters in your life. There are always going to be negative experiences in your life and mindfulness helps you to see these experiences as potential learning opportunities instead of being the bleak situations you first saw.

How often you need reminding of the wideness of the world or the beauty that it offers you is down to individual choice. Personally, even now, after teaching for many years, this gives me extra strength and allows me to feel Mother Nature looking over me or sharing her fruits with me. It also makes me feel honored to have the ability to use all my senses to their intended purpose. Enjoy your senses. They help you to trust yourself more and you will find that you will start using intuition and being able to listen to it when you give yourself that kind of space from the negativity of life.

You won't learn everything straight away. Meditation and mindfulness take time to become part and parcel of your life. You may be reading a book and suddenly find yourself transfixed by the location of the book or the characters in the story. Mindfulness helps you to be in that moment and it gives rich reward. I remember one day doing something terribly mundane and actually finding myself feeling very happy doing it because it helped to quieten the moment, regardless of how much I always detested doing that job. Now, I use mindfulness all of the time each day of my life to allow that quietness to take place, which frees up the imagination and allows the subconscious to feel and enjoy the silence imposed.

Chapter 18: The Power Of Gratitud

The power that is held within gratitude is something we all know is there, if we take the time to really look. We are all made of energy and this energy vibrated at a very high level. This high level is also known as love.

When we connect to this high level we become very different people. Our attitudes change, we act very differently. This is all because we are following our natural state of being. Gratitude is one with love. It is a high vibration and because of the Law of Correspondence, it has a counterpart. When people are ungrateful, they are pushing against their natural state of being. People do this when they hold onto hatred, rage, jealousy, anger, or any negative emotion. The reason that feels so awful is because they are closing off their true thoughts or their true mindfulness. Their inner being is filled with love and wanting to give this love but their egos want to hold onto bitterness. This can manifest into physical illness or general uncomfortableness in the body.

Being grateful for the Now moment

When we are always hoping for a better future or dwelling too much on the past and what once was, we are forgetting one important this—the now. This very moment is the moment you want to focus on. Be aware of your body, your mind, and how your soul feels. Be aware of your emotions and what they want to tell you. Be aware of your body and where it hurts. It all means something. If we are constantly in the past or in the future we are showing the Universe that we are ungrateful for the beauty of this moment and where we are now. This moment has been created because of all our past experiences and there is greatness in what it holds but sometimes we just need to look a little deeper.

Being present in the moment

It's important to take time and show gratitude to where we are now and there are a few ways that we can do this. Some techniques work better for others depending on the individual but they are all worth exploring to see what's best for you.

Gratitude List

We can do gratitude lists two different ways. We can either take time in the morning or evening to write out what we are grateful for in the day (or the day before) or keep a notebook with us to record our gratitude as we go. Some find that if their day is busy it is easier to get grounded after a long day and take time out to write about the amazing things that happened in their day whilst others find it more rewarding to write down things after they happened as a way of savoring the moment. Not only that, because of the Law of Attraction, the more we notice these amazing things, the more of them we'll really start to see in our day.

Showing others appreciation

Being grateful towards others can leave us feeling amazing. When we take time out to say thank you in a unique way or to just show something that we noticed their efforts, we feel great. This is because we are acting as our inner being does and showing love which really just connects us to the Universe.

When we do this we see it reflected back to us. When we show gratitude we receive gratitude back. This is because of the Law of Compensation. What we put out to the Universe we receive it back two fold. If we want to receive more help in our lives we have to become the source of it and give it. This is when we get it back. We can also do this for material gain like financial abundance. If we want more money we must give money away. Helping others who don't have as much as us or someone who just needs a helping hand will cause the Universe to multiply it and give it back to us.

Simple Tips:

·Show gratitude to those around you whenever you can

·Always show gratitude to yourself after you take action on something

·Write down all that you are grateful for each night

·Write out a list of what you're grateful for in others and show it to them

·Be grateful that you have money when you spend it

·Show gratitude for the foods you eat and water you drink

Chapter 19: Mindful Living

How to integrate mindfulness into everyday living

Realizing that you are the creator of all that you experience may be a bit daunting at first. But the fact is that this realization is probably the most empowering thing you can come to learn about yourself. You hold the power to consciously create your experience within every moment, through awareness of yourself, your mind and your perceptions.

We have always been creating something for ourselves, so this is nothing new. If practiced with genuine integrity, mindfulness can bring about incredible transformations in our everyday lives, very rapidly and efficiently.

Here are some tips for mindful living:

1. Wake up and start your day with the mindset you wish to have for the rest of

the day. As you wake up in the morning, whether still in your bed or meditating on the floor, think of what you would like to experience and the person you would like to be today. Affirm that you are happy, fulfilled, prosperous, excited, blessed and thankful. Enter your day with a sense of excitement to be alive.

2. Know and understand that you have the freedom of choice and creation in every moment. In each moment, become aware that you have the choice to choose the reality you wish to experience. You have the choice to be frustrated or happy. You have the choice to be anxious or calm. You have the choice to eat junk food or fill your body with healthy food. You have the power to choose to be positive. You can be happy to be alive – you simply have to choose to do so. When you become mindful of this power of decision that you have, you can and will create the reality that you would like to experience.

3. Become aware of the effect you have on yourself, the people around you and

your environment. When we are mindful, we can stop to think about the impact

of our thoughts, our words, our actions. We can begin to shape our impact on others and the world around us. Do we walk into a room and immediately start shouting and causing unrest? How is this affecting the people in that situation? How is it making them feel? Do we criticize ourselves and others? Are we proud of who we are? Do we sabotage ourselves through the things we eat, say and do? Are we the person we want to be? Are we conscious of our environment? Do we litter? Do we recycle? Do we take responsibility for our actions? Do we inspire and motivate others? Do we share love and happiness? These are all things that we should be aware of in our day-to-day lives, because everything we do creates the reality we experience and affects the lives of those around us.

4. Shift from a negative to a positive state of existence. In every moment we have a choice as to what to feel, think, say and

do. And by becoming aware of this, we realize that we have the power in every moment to choose a positive response over a negative response. This can be extremely hard at times. Perhaps there is someone at work who just gets on your nerves because they will not stop talking to you. This can make your life at work very difficult, so what do you do? Shout at them and tell them how annoying they are? This will upset both of you, and only increase the tension between the two of you for every moment to come. They are only annoying because you perceive them to be so, so whose fault is that? Or do you take a deep breath, accept them and the situation, smile at them and gently ask them to stop talking as you find it hard to concentrate? By acting from a place of love, we liberate ourselves from hate, frustration, anxiety and anger. We become able to live each moment in a state of positivity, love, peace and harmony. And, most importantly, we can allow others to be who they truly are.

5. The gift of gratitude is the most powerful tool that we can use to find

fulfillment in each moment. Gratitude will help to bring you into the present and immediately shift you from a negative to a positive state of mind. Many of us wake up and immediately think of work and everything that has to be done in the day. We start to feel anxious by all that is expected of us during the course of the day. But when we shift our perception to a state of gratitude and focus on all that we are and all that we have, we immediately focus on all the positives. Gratitude is one of the most incredible tools we can use to shift ourselves from a feeling of lack to a feeling of abundance, a state not defined by the amount of things we have – but rather a state of happiness and fulfillment. Gratitude also

Chapter 20: Breaking Free From Your Past

Are you a victim of a past event? If you have ever lost a loved one, had your heart broken or had trouble in school you may find it difficult to let go and move on. Learn how to take back your life - the past is the past. There are methods to move on and cope. If you do not learn how to move on the past will overtake your life. When you learn how to let go of the past and move on you will be happier, not as worried feel the pain no longer. You can learn to let go of the past and move on! When you truly learn how to move on from the past, you can truly experience the love, joy and peace life has to offer.

The first step in moving is to feel your emotions. Yell, cry or scream if you feel like it. If you feel down allow yourself to be down. Whatever you do the key is to not hide from your feelings. Avoiding how you feel will only make matters worse. If you are feeling sad - cry, call a friend and cry, take a bath and cry. Feel your pain if you are angry. Venting and crying are good for you; it helps you to release the emotions. Share your feelings with a trusted friend or see a counselor. When you experience your emotions, you can let go of the past and move on.

Forgiveness is the second step to moving off from the past. Forgive yourself and others of the mistakes that have been made. One of the keys to moving on is forgiveness. You don't have to forget to be able to forgive. But, you will never move on if you do not forgive. If you have said something you should not have - forgive yourself. If you were not there for someone - forgive yourself. If someone has betrayed or wronged you - forgive them. Forgive yourself and other and let go of the past and move on.

Acceptance is the third step in letting go of the past and moving on. Accept your loss, accept your pain, accept the broken heart. With acceptance, you are on your way to freeing yourself from the past. We can learn from our experiences and the past, but the past is the past. If you live in the present moment, you have the future to look forward to. Accept that you have been disappointed, embarrassed or heartbroken and allowed yourself to heal and grow.

The last key to moving on from the past is to live. Live for the hope of something new without fear. Live a life of happiness and joy, live for those you've lost, live life without regrets. In living a full life, you will let go of the past. Help others get over past experiences similar to yours. Living your life does not mean that past events did not happen, but, you do not have to give up you can move on, and live for today and look forward to the future.

There is no individual that hasn't experienced pain or sadness as this is a normal thing in life. However, some stay living in the past for a long time. As life goes on, it becomes harder for them to overcome these negative feelings that they experienced and can end up in depression. When the individual keeps living in the past, he could be hurting his emotions, current relationships with others, lose focus, and become a procrastinator.

Some people wait for the new year to start making resolutions and new changes in their lives. What they don't realize that every day is a new day and can be used for change. If you want to free yourself from the past, you shouldn't wait for a new year; you can start right now.

Holding on to the sadness and pain from the past is harmful since you will be focusing on the negative emotions, instead of focusing on the emotions of happiness. To overcome the sadness and depression that you acquired, you need to free yourself from the past and focus on the present time.

You might be saying I want to live free from the past and move on with your life, but don't know how. To learn how to become free from the past, follow the quick guide below:

1. Express your inner feelings

Talk to someone about the pain and sadness you feel. Expressing your emotions and venting helps to relax you. Don't be shy to talk to someone about your pain and sadness. Talk and complain until you get everything out of your heart, so with time, you can move forward.

2. Decide to live in the present

"If you pay attention to the present, you can improve upon it. And, if you improve on the present what comes later will also be better." -Paulo Coelho

Realize how living in the past is hurting you. Ask yourself, how it is affecting you? Is it affecting your relationship with others? Is it affecting your career? Is it affecting your health? If the answer is yes to these questions, then decide to free yourself from the past. Decide to take care of yourself first and you can do that by living in the present and by focusing on the positive qualities you have in your life.

3. You have a choice

You can't control the actions of others, but you can control your thoughts and actions. You can commit to stopping focusing on the bad experiences of the past and the pain you have. Choose to move forward and not backward.

4. Know your responsibilities

Know that you were part of the event and situation and you could have done something to avoid what happened in the past. This doesn't mean you are to blame, but you have to realize that you are not the victim, but you are a person who is a participant in life and its events like everyone else.

5. Forgiveness

Forgiveness will change your life for the better. However, forgiveness doesn't mean that you have to forget what has happened completely. What you have to do is forgive, so you can overcome the pain, anger, and sadness you hold from the past.

6. Acceptance

Accept the past completely. The past helps you to learn from and gain experiences. Acceptance is the key to getting away from the past and moving on with your life. You are on the way to freedom if you accept what can't be changed.

Chapter 21: How Mindfulness Helps With Everyday Problems

You may be wondering how mindfulness can help you with everyday problems. Before we go into detail about meditation, which we have reiterated in different parts of this book, let's show you how mindfulness helps you to become a better person – able to deal with day to day problems. You may be wondering what the connection is between mindfulness and overcoming the kinds of problems people face today. There's a huge connection and you need to understand this to gain the most from mindfulness.

When you become mindful, you also appreciate that negativity makes your life more difficult and consciously put to one side any sense of judgment on situations. What does this mean? It means, you have no room for the following elements:

- Anger
- Grudges

- Jealousy
- Greed
- Loathing

The only thing you should be mindful about when it comes to negative experiences and emotions is that they are detrimental to your life. Thus, mindfulness puts these aside and when you are able to do that, you actually enhance your life considerably. Instead of being angry and judgmental, you begin to look at situations in a different way. For example, if my wife says something that is uncalled for and nasty, I use mindfulness to help me see beyond it instead of getting angry. If you look beyond all of the things that are negative, you get to see the bigger picture and you are much more able to accept what is happening in your life.

Let's give you an example. In the opening of this book, I told you a story about my daughter being ill in hospital and having to choose between work and her. My boss was indignant about taking time off from work to be with my daughter. Instead of being angry toward him, with mindfulness in my heart, I would have seen that it was actually sad that he could not see beyond what was needed at work. I could and chose my daughter. At the time that all of this was happening, I was threatened with losing my job, I had a daughter whose medical bills would cost a fortune and had no one else to turn to. In that moment of reality, I looked at the situation in the way that mindful people do. Here are the realities:

- My daughter was sick

- My job needed me but would not collapse without me

- My daughter's medical bills would need paying

- If I lost my job, I could keep my medical cover sufficiently long to see her through

Then I had to look at other scenarios in my life and see whether my decisions were correct or not, based on my current beliefs and mindfulness practice. In many cases, the only time that wrong decisions were involved was when there was also negativity. When I looked at good decisions that I had been proud of making, none of these had any negativity attached to them.

In your life, you need to adopt mindfulness because it reminds you of your real status in life, regardless of what emotions are telling you. For example, it helps to balance the mind and not make rash decisions based upon negative emotions. The moment that I saw clearly that my daughter's health was the only thing I needed to concern myself with, I dropped all the negativity I had felt and made the right decision and it can happen for you too.

Imagine this case scenario. You are angry with someone for something thoughtless that he/she has said to you. You allow the thought to fester within your mind. All of the time that you do that, what you are doing is missing the opportunity to live in that moment in time. Thus, moment after moment passes, totally wasted on negative thoughts toward another human being. You haven't actually gained anything from that time of anger. All you did was waste the opportunity of enjoying a moment or two in your life by letting negativity overshadow everything else.

How to deal with anger

In a case where something angers you, you need to be able to see things from another perspective. In Buddhist practice, a Buddhist observes what happens without judging it and without taking any negativity from the situation. Try to do the same. When someone angers you, smile at them and show that you are not prepared to be drawn into their negativity. Give ownership of that negativity to them. In some situations it may be less appropriate to smile and this may be perceived as smugness. In those situations, simply be glad that you are you and don't judge the person for being him/herself. If that person has expressed anger or has said something thoughtless, show that it does not affect you but that you are merely an observer. Let the negativity stay with that person. It is only when you allow it to penetrate your thoughts that you actually get affected by it and take tranquility out of the picture.

Step away from anger and find humility and empathy. Empathy is greatly misunderstood by many to mean understanding, but it's much more than that. When you empathize, you actually make the effort to put yourself into someone else's shoes and see things from their angle or point of view. When you are able to do that, you lose the need for anger and feel sorry that friends who would normally provoke anger are failing in themselves and want to bring you down with them. Be compassionate and understanding instead of falling into the trap of anger and it will pass.

Your children are in trouble

The instant response of a parent is to want to help the child. Whether the child wants to be helped may be another thing entirely. As parents, people are faced with having to make decisions every day of their lives and these may not be decisions that they choose to make. It's just that life throws curve balls and parents have to come up with solutions. When I started to apply mindfulness into my life, when children came to me with their problems, I asked them to sit down so that I was giving them my full attention. Often, we listen to kids from a distance and don't really understand the extent of their worries. In that moment where all your attention is given to the child, you can really learn to listen to what a child is saying. Remember the code. Listen – absorb – do not judge. With mindful thought you can help your child work out his/her own problem without throwing judgmental parenthood down their throats.

Child: I stole someone's pocket money and I feel bad about it.

Parent: What do you think you should do to make it right?

Child: I don't know.

Parent: Well I can see a couple of alternatives. Look harder and see what you see.

Child: I could give it back but I spent some of it

Parent: How long will it take you to save that much?

Child: About a week if I do all my chores

Parent: So what's the answer?

Child: Give back what I have, say sorry and promise him the rest when I get my pocket money.

Parent: And that's really what you want to do?

Child: Yes.

In this case scenario there is no judgment and there doesn't need to be any. The child already feels bad about what he/she did and is regretting it. The child has learned that the consequence may be losing that friend and is scared to tell the friend, but with the backing of the parent can do that, knowing that his intentions are to repay the debt.

This may not be a typical scenario but the way that the parent listens without judgment is vital to the picture. Mindfulness means looking at problems and distancing yourself from them in order to find a solution. The opposite of this is for the parent to get angry with the child and make his guilt even heavier than it already is and that doesn't make sense — though many parents do this.

These moments that you have with your children are creeping by. They are just moments in time and you need to use your mindfulness to actually be aware of what's happening with your child and perhaps point in the right direction occasionally when the child loses focus on what's right and what's wrong.

Chapter 22: Practising Body Scan

You are now in the second day of this 7 days' mindfulness journey for self-discovery and enhancing own self-confidence ultimately; today, you will be doing physical body scanning meditation. We have already established that the process of engaging in mindful breathing which is regarded as breathing meditation during the first day of the mindfulness journey. In breathing meditation, you observe what goes on around and within you not with the intention to alter anything but to gain understanding and discover yourself through simply observing your own breathing. We able to use our breathing as a means of relieve from stress and anxiety.

Now you will be working on your body to become aware of it. This session will take approximately 6 minutes. If possible, make effort to continue the exercise beyond the first week in order to get amazing results. A 7 days' Mindfulness practice is a good start towards the result you desire but you can achieve more when you continue the practice. Mindfulness is the art of living in the moment; it is an enjoyable life journey. So, if you are dealing with stress and desire to enhance your confidence which is essential for success in any domains or industries, then you may consider to make Mindfulness your way of life.

2nd days' practice is a body scan exercise, it is simply taking notice of any sensation in your physical body at this present moment. Your present thought will affect your body. Be mindful that body scan practice may not be relaxing but you will relax eventually. Just feel, let it be and relax.

Notice your body

Do you notice how you respond to certain feeling especially emotional pain? Have you ever been in an uncomfortable situation before? The normal reaction we have for such feelings is to avoid, escape or to get rid of the pain or discomfort. But have you ever thought of accepting the pain or discomfort? The truth is that, pain and any other kind of undesirable feelings can be accepted and used to your advantage; this may sound impossible but it will be when you stop judging it and let it take its course like a river flow through the place where the pain is, be still and watch it goes by. Soon, you will find it no more.

In the animals' world, when an animal gets hurt, it will find a quiet place and be still and rest; human being somehow forgotten the feeling of being still and rest, thus feel your breathing, learn to feel the presence of your body and pay attention to any feelings and sensation of various parts of your body such as feet, hands, face, thighs, arm, shoulder, and even your muscles.

Here, we start the body scan practice:

2nd Day's Practice

Begin by bringing your attention to your body.

You may close your eyes, if it is more comfortable for you.

You may notice your body weight on the chair or on where you are seated.

Take a deep breath. Breathe-in slowly and breathe-out slowly.

Take another deep breath. Feel the air in and out of your nose.

Continue to take a few deep breaths.

As you inhale, you are bringing all the goodness to the body.

As you exhale, you are breathing out all toxic and unwanted stuffs out of your body.

You will soon have a sense of relaxation in your body and it continue to grow.

You may notice your feet on the floor and notice the sensations of your feet touching the floor.

Notice your weight on the chair.

Notice the clothe that touches your skin. Take your time.

Notice the sensation around your stomach, your chest, your shoulder, your hands, your neck, your mouth, your nose, your ear and your forehead.

Notice if any discomforts come with the sensation.

Acknowledge the discomfort, saying: "This is how I feel", if there is any.

Relax your body and allow it to go soften.

Notice the rising and falling of your chest and your stomach.

Soften your jaw. Allow your face and facial muscles to be soft.

Notice your body in the room you are in. Sense your own presence.

Take one deep breath, inhale 4-3-2-1, exhale 6-5-4-3-2-1.

Take another deep breath, inhale 4-3-2-1 and exhale 6-5-4-3-2-1.

When you are ready, you can open your eyes and notice you are back in the room.

INTERACTING WITH EXTERNAL WORLD

Today we will learn on how to interact with the external world mindfully. The exercise is simple and can be completed in a few minutes. Feel free to continue with the practice in your own comfortable way and stop whenever you want.

Every working adult knows what it takes to be professional in one's job. The price to pay may be managing tonnes of stress and sacrificing personal time with family and friends. The work demands in the modern world, in our society, are weighing heavily on our shoulders. How to live in peace with the world outside? We do not need to know how, we just need to let go and breathe. Your body knows how to inhale and it knows how to exhale; you need to exhale at time.

Most of the time we are so caught up with the demands of work that we hardly notice what are going on around us. A mindfulness practice on interacting with external world will help you to gain more awareness of your immediate environment which in turn will make you more flexible as you adapt to different working conditions in the office.

3rd Day's Practice

We will be doing the following exercises to sharper our awareness of the surrounding by noticing what is around us. Take your time to go through them one by one. So, if you are ready, let's start:

Sight: Look around you and name the 1st object as you look for 5 different objects, then do the same for the 2nd object out of those 5 objects, then the 3rd object out of those 5 objects and so on (example: blue book, red shirt, white watch, green leave, purple cup).

Sight & Touch: Look, name and touch 5 different objects, noticing their texture, temperature, mass and weight as you do so. Similarly, start with the 1st object, then do the same for the 2nd object, the 3rd object, the 4th object and lastly the 5th object.

Sight, Touch and Smell/Taste: Look at (things around you), name, taste and smell

5 different objects, noticing their colours, texture, taste and aroma. Start with the 1st object, then do the same for 2nd object, 3rd object till you complete the practice for all 5 objects.

Hearing: Close your eyes and listen for 5 different sounds. Count 5-4-3-2-1.

Take time and do the above exercise for two rounds. Practise breathing technique after each exercise: breathe-in count (silently) 4-3-2-1, hold breath count (silently) 2-1, breathe-out count (silently) 4-3-2-1. You are ready for your next challenge.

Chapter 23: Mindfulness For Stress

Stress and anxiety are the most common life problems in today's world. However it is our belief that a majority of stresses that we experience are self-inflicted. Yes you read it right. We choose to be stressed.

This might sound odd but we actually have a choice over the sort of stresses that we bring into our lives. We are not referring to the obvious work or relationships related stresses but the kind that we experience everyday without taking any notice of it.

Imagine a simple scenario. You're stuck in a traffic jam and the man behind you is constantly honking. Negative thoughts flood your mind. You throw curses at him, both verbally and silently but since you can apparently do nothing about it, you let the sound get over your nerves. You let yourself stress out by imagining scenarios through which to get back at him for this bad behaviour. However you know that you cannot do anything about the situation. The incapability to act gets on your nerves and as a result, you become discontented and stressful.

You might have missed it, but you actually had a choice in the above mentioned scenario. The choice is not to ignore the loud obscene noise but to actively concentrate elsewhere.

Imagine it this way, that right now there are many background noises going on behind you. People might be chatting, someone might be typing, birds might be chirping and so on. However since you are reading this book, your concentration is fully absorbed in comprehending the meaning of these words. You are aware of the noises in your background but your active concentration is consumed somewhere else hence you don't even notice the background sounds.

Feeling astound? Your brain is a wonderful organ. However most people allow the impressions that they have formed throughout their lives to control their actions. They are not controlling their brain but rather their memory is.

Psychologists have found that a set of people respond similarly to a specific set of stimuli. This is so because they have fed their brain the appropriate responses to certain conditions. For example, a teacher has led him/herself into believing that he/she should be offended if a student questions the credibility of the facts stated in the lecture. Being offended might not actually be the real response but rather the automatic reaction carried out by your memory.

Renowned psychiatrist Viktor Frankl said; "Between stimulus and response there's a space, in that space lies our power to choose our response, in our response lies our growth and our freedom."

In other words, we allow undue stresses in our lives because we hand over the control of this space to our memories. We do not utilize this space to make active, concentrated decisions but rather act upon a set of responses our brain fed us.

We are once again suffering because we are dwelling in the past. Mindfulness guides us to live in the present. To react to situations as they were new and just happening now and to not let previous experiences cloud over what is happening today.

University of Massachusetts Medical Centre introduced the Mindfulness Based Stress Reduction Program in 1979. The program was initiated by Jon Kabat-Zinn. It is an eight week program that helps chronic patients to be more mindful of the activities and responses of their body. It combines mindfulness with yoga to actually repair and heal the body. The group meets once a week to practice various targeted yoga poses with an active concentration towards the responses of the body with each fluid movement.

Since its inauguration in 1979, Mindfulness Based Stress Reduction Program has shown great promise and progress. Many chronic patients who have followed the program closely and have moulded their lives to be more mindful have shown great progress. The program guides patients and students on how to deal with negative emotions and reactions.

Each one of us is different. Hence what brings forth the inner strain is different for all of us. The approach of being mindful appreciates this individuality. Any program or teacher can only guide you. The journey is however yours alone.

In the meantime, there has been tremendous research on the effectiveness of Mindfulness Based Stress Reduction Program. Research hosted by Harvard and Stanford has shown that being mindful is so much helpful in reducing stress levels and living a more fulfilled life. Not only does it negate the negative mental effects of stress but also helps in reducing the harmful physical effects linked with stress. These include high blood pressure and the associated heart problems.

Even just now, if you just take a deep breath and make an active concentrated effort to not let the situation control you,

you'd be surprised at how much more content and relaxed you feel.

Chapter 24: Benefits Of Neuroplasticity And Positive Thinking

Research on neuroplasticity has become so popular in recent days, especially among the leading psychiatrists. Neuroplasticity in psychiatry is a concept that is spreading like wildfire. This has created a huge impact on various treatments for ailments like depression, schizophrenia, anxiety, substance abuse, and several other major health conditions that are treated by expert psychiatrists.

The power of positive thinking. How many times have you heard that phrase thrown around? It's so much a part of our vernacular now that it's almost become meaningless. We'd all agree that thinking positively is a good thing. Especially when we're feeling positive.

But what about when things are bad? What about those days when you're so stressed that you can't even think straight? What about those days when you are taken off guard by multiple events that completely beat you into submission.

Most of us have met people who remain extremely upbeat during really bad times. Just between you and me, it makes me want to slap them sometimes. That whimsical, "life is beautiful" attitude when things are imploding really used to get under my skin. But I've come to learn that these people knew something I didn't.

Here's the secret that's not even a secret anymore. It's revolutionary, thrilling science. Positive thinking actually changes your brain, and not in some hippy, woo-woo kind of way; it changes your brain in a physical way.

The science is called neuroplasticity. It means that the thoughts we think are able to actually change the structure and function of our brains. The idea of neuroplasticity was first introduced in 1890 by William James, and it was vehemently rejected by scientists who as a whole believed that the brain is rigidly mapped, with certain parts of the brain controlling certain functions. They all said if that part died or was damaged, the function was to be altered or lost entirely. Well, it's starting to look like they were dead wrong.

Neuroplasticity is now widely accepted, as scientists start to prove that the brain is forever adaptable and malleable.

The brain retains the power to change its own structure, and this holds true even for those with severe neurological ailments. Those with problems like strokes, cerebral palsy, and mental illness can literally different areas of their brains through repetitive mental and physical activities. This science is proving to be completely life-altering.

But what does this have to do with positive thinking?

This means repetitive positive thought and repetitive positive activity can rewire your brain. It strengthens certain areas in the brain areas that stimulate positive feelings.

In his groundbreaking book, The Brain That Changes Itself: Stories of Personal Triumph from the Frontiers of Brain Science, Norman Doidge M.D. says straight out that the brain has the capacity to rewire itself and/or form new neural pathways — if we put in the work. It's just like exercise: the work requires repetition and activity to reinforce new learning.

Here are some actions you can take to change your own brain during the bad times.

Fearing Failure

Almost all of us fear doing something new; we don't wait to fail. The fact of the matter is, we can do most anything granted we take action, quit negative thinking, and change our perceptions of the truth about our abilities.

Action steps:

Make yourself stop thinking about all of the reasons you can't do something, even if you don't feel courageous or entirely capable. The moment that a negative thought creeps in, reroute your brain into thinking a positive thought about your ability instead. Then take small actions each day toward achieving your goal or desired change.

Over-thinking/Worrying:

How many times have you felt trapped in obsessive over-thinking about a problem or in a state of anxiety or worry that lasts for days or even weeks? It robs you of energy, ruins your sleep, and tanks your mood and overall outlook on life in general. Obsessing over your problem only strengthens the worry function in your brain.

Action steps:

When you find yourself in the cycle of worry or compulsive thinking, apply the three R's — rename, re-frame, and redirect. As the moment that worry begins, mentally scream "Stop!" Rename the issue by reminding yourself that worry isn't real. Rename it as a kneejerk reaction, not a reality. Re-frame your thinking by focusing on positive or distracting thoughts, whether or not you still feel anxious. Force your mind to think other thoughts. Redirect your actions. Go do something inspiring and exciting, fun or mentally engaging. The real gold is in following these steps repeatedly, every time you are anxious or worrying obsessively, to break the pattern and rewire your brain.

Mood Disorders/Phobias

Sometimes we might just feel blue or out-of-sorts, and it's just a temporary state of mind that settles in and goes away after a couple days. But some mood disorders, like depression or serious anxieties that turn into phobias, can be disabling and unrelenting. Psychologists and behavioral therapists have used treatments based on neuroplasticity to get to the cognitive root of these problems and put a patient's life back on track.

Action steps:

A serious mood disorder or phobia requires the help of a trained counselor. Cognitive behavioral therapy (CBT) is a type of treatment that helps people learn how to identify and change negative thought patterns that have an influence on behavior and mood. If you suffer from severe anxiety or depression, you need someone skilled to help you get to the root of these thoughts and to show you how to change them. Ask them about CBT.

Scientists are now looking at neuroplasticity to approach a wide variety of cognitive problems and disorders including:

Loss of senses — vision, balance and hearing

Learning disorders and reading problems

Auditory processing problems

Autism and hypersensitivity

The aging brain and memory

Issues related to love and sex

Stroke and brain injury recovery

Cerebral palsy

Chronic pain

Obsessive compulsive disorder

Psychological trauma

Depression and anxiety

Cognitive problems after brain surgery

Neuroplasticity and anxiety cure

The concept behind neuroplasticity is that brain cells keep remodeling themselves throughout our life span. Other research proves that brain cells of people suffering from anxiety get damaged day by day, leading to negative plasticity. Scientists have tried and correlated these two findings in order to research on how neuroplasticity can help in such disorders. Practicing neuroplasticity and forming consistent positive thinking and neural pathways has redeemed and helped recover from brain cell damages caused by anxiety.

Neuroplasticity and Depression

Many people who have undergone a tragic experience feel total despair, loneliness and they possess a sense of hopelessness. They reach a stage of acute depression where they do not share anything with anyone and live in a separate world. They might just keep quite or talk irrelevantly. Reasons behind this stage of depression might be countless. It might be due to some accident or death of loved ones, or a break up, or sudden losses in business or any other traumatic experience. The main effect of such depressive moods is damaging to brain cells. This can be curbed and positivity can be induced into our brains through the practice of neuroplasticity. Studies and experiments have proved very good results in treating patients with acute depression by method of neuroplastic therapy.

Chapter 25: When To Practice Mindfulness?

When you practice mindfulness is up to individual taste. While certain schools of thought believe that certain types of meditation should be done at certain times of day, at certain locations and in certain ways; for the purpose of this book and your mindfulness practice, we will not bother ourselves as much with those details. Instead, I would ask that you consider when, throughout the day, you would most benefit from practicing something that is intended to help you relieve stress, relax, and focus. The most common answer that I have heard to that question is "in the morning before work" or before starting your day. This is often the recommendation from mindfulness practitioners and they even say that they use their time of mindfulness to plan out and create how they want their day to develop. At first, this may sound ridiculous, like some kind of manifest destiny, but many people start the day by deciding for themselves if they want their day to be filled with happiness, surprise, and interest, or that they going to let the day become something full of anger or frustration. This act of deciding to be happy or deciding to be interested in things throughout your day will set you up to be mindful of the things that you want to happen as the day goes on. A good example of this comes from Richard Bach's book called "Illusions: Adventures of a Reluctant Messiah" where the main character is asked to manifest something in his day. At first he just imagines what he wants to see, but as the day goes on and he is having lunch, he sees on the side of a bottle a blue feather and becomes excited when he notices that what he tried to manifest was a bluebird. What he was doing was preparing his mind to be mindfully aware of the things he would like to see from his day and when they presented themselves, he was more able to notice and acknowledge them. While he may not have literally created a bluebird, was able to notice the feather where he might not have been able to normally.

We can start our day in such a way as well. Think about wanting to see someone "be nice" or wanting to see something positive or wanting to learn something new. Whatever it is we prepare our mind to see, we will be more likely to see it in our world. The cautionary note here is we can also do this for negative thoughts and images as well. If I start my day by saying "today is going to be a bad day," chances are I will only be able to see the negative happenings of the day and completely miss all the positive things I encounter. Does all this mean that you need to have a mindful practice in the morning? Of course not, I'd be contradicting myself in that case. This is just one option and one way you can utilize it. Other options include evenings after work even during your drive home. This is a great time to practice mindfulness before returning home to your family! On another note, a question that often comes up in my therapy practice is "how often and how long should I do it?" Every 30 minutes? Every hour? I have read a lot of articles that suggested even just 10 minutes of mindfulness practice per day improves people's mood throughout the day. So what's my suggestion? I suggest you practice between 15 and 30 minutes of mindfulness actively throughout your day, any time of day you can make time for it, on a daily basis. I once heard a quote stating that "if you don't have 10 minutes to practice mindfulness, you need to do 20 minutes of mindfulness."

Conclusion

Mindfulness is a state of mind that allows you to be a happier, kinder, and more positive person. Through mindfulness, you can find the true secrets behind true and lasting happiness. You will truly be living your life to the fullest through mindful living. Your concepts on what happiness and how you can achieve it will change during your practice and you can pursue true wisdom.

As you delve deeper into mindfulness, you will find yourself developing more meaningful relationships, become more optimistic, and be able to cherish each moment as it comes. Start your mindful meditation practice with optimism and commitment and you will surely go far.

Be ready to live life to the fullest!

www.ingramcontent.com/pod-product-compliance
Lightning Source LLC
Chambersburg PA
CBHW072011070526
44583CB00015B/1429